NO MORE SMALL TALK

By

SCOTTIE FRASER

the Peppertree Press
www.peppertreepublishing.com

ISBN: 978-1-61493-946-7

Library of Congress: 2024908395

Printed: April 2024

Manufactured in the United State of America

Dedication

This book is dedicated to the many U.S. voters who feel cheated because they are disenchanted with the presidential nominees selected by the political parties, and feel compelled on Election Day to vote, if they vote at all, for the nominee they consider least undesirable.

Table of Contents

Introduction

The 2024 presidential election is less than a year away. Who will be the presidential nominees? How will they be chosen? Why were they chosen? Who will you vote for on Election Day? Why?

As of January 1, 2024, the polls tell us Joe Biden will be the probable nominee of the Democratic Party. And as of the same date, the polls tell us Donald Trump will be the probable nominee of the Republican Party. The two squared off against each other in the 2020 presidential election. Joe Biden was formally declared the winner.

"Not so," according to Donald Trump. Regardless of the generally accepted election results, Trump and his Make America Great Again (MAGA) supporters assert that he was robbed of the presidency by reason of "election fraud." Most people, including other Republicans, disagree with Trump's assertions. Nevertheless, the 2020 election is over. It's in the books. Joe Biden is our president.

Though Biden and Trump presently are the front-runners for the 2024 election, there are challengers. Though still early in the nominating process, six Republican contenders other than Trump are vying for the nomination, including Ron DeSantis, governor of Florida; Nikki Haley, former South Carolina governor and later United Nations ambassador; Chris Christie, former governor of New Jersey; Asa Hutchinson, former Arkansas governor; and Vivek Ramaswamy, a Yale-Harvard-schooled entrepreneur from Ohio.

On the Democratic side, in addition to President Biden, Vice President Kamala Harris, is waiting in the wings to see how receptive Democratic voters are to a second term for President Biden. Marianne Williamson, an author and spiritual advisor, is also a remote option to being the nominee. Others, not readily identifiable now, might enter the Democratic primaries.

West Virginia Democrat Senator Joe Manchin announced he would not be seeking re-election to the Senate seat he presently occupies. He has allowed his name to be circulated as a possible nominee of the recently established No Labels Party. The No Labels Party was created in 2023 to consider nominating a candidate to oppose Biden and Trump, with the hope of capturing enough votes from Independents and moderate-leaning voters to win the election. Manchin and the No Labels Party are well aware that third-party presidential candidates in the past have had no success in being elected—except for Teddy Roosevelt in 1915.

Neither President Biden nor former President Trump is a "spring chicken," as Trump is 78 years old, while Biden is 81. Both are vulnerable to assertions by challengers and voters that neither is mentally or physically fit to handle the demands of the presidency for a four-year term. Age will be a factor in the next presidential election. How much? Time will tell. Trump has made Biden's fitness to serve a major campaign issue. Democrats, but not Biden, point out that Trump also has made several of his own age-related gaffes and verbal inaccuracies. Governor DeSantis thinks both Biden and Trump are too old to endure the stress presidents generally experience when under pressure.

A list of concerns the next president must address should include: immigration, particularly what's happening now at our southern border; the ongoing territorial dispute between the Israelis and Palestinians over land now occupied by both in the Mideast; the high level of tension between Jews and Palestinians on college campuses here and abroad—testing the constitutional limits of Freedom of Speech; Iran's involvement in the Israeli-Palestinian conflict through its support of Hamas; Russia's invasion of Ukraine; the use of nuclear weapons; exploration and control of outer-space; sources of energy; and multiple budget issues.

Is Biden or Trump qualified to represent the United States in making decisions regarding these important matters? How would we know if neither talk about them during the campaign. Do voters demand that the nominees publicly address these important matters so that they can make more informed decisions when voting on Election Day? I don't think so! Do the voters really care what the nominees think on most issues affecting our way of life?

Unfortunately, when Election Day arrives, far too many persons haven't a clue how the nominee for whom they will vote will address these important national and global issues. Why not? Because nominees would rather not have their thoughts on controversial issues known for fear of losing votes—and possibly the election. And why should nominees risk asserting a position on important controversial issues when the public doesn't seem to care?

So when it comes time to vote (if they vote at all), registered voters typically vote the party line. Registered Democratic voters tend to vote for the Democratic nominee, while registered Republican voters are inclined to vote for the Republican nominee. The wild card in a presidential election is the Independent vote.

Not good! The President is a very important person. In addition to being the elected leader of the United States, he wears many other hats, including chief U.S. policy maker and Commander-in-Chief of the U.S. Military Forces.

Shouldn't a country such as ours have an election process that offers voters an opportunity to select a person to be president based on how that person addresses the issues deemed important to the public? Shouldn't we voters demand that any person vying to be president earns our votes by convincing us how he or she will lead our country for the next four years and maybe more? Is party-line voting the best we can do in selecting the leader of our country?

No More Small Talk addresses these thoughts in a style that challenges traditional thinking about the presidential election process. This book is not intended to persuade people about what to think on critical national and global matters. However, it is intended to point out that voters are the presidential electors and as such, they have an inherent obligation to select as our president a person who has convinced us of how he or she will address national and global issues that concern our country.

CHAPTER 1

The Trip Home:
The End of the Campaign
6/30/2024

★ ★ ★

Hugo understood that delivering a speech in Madison Square Garden to a packed audience consisting mostly of New Yorkers, including many Jews and Palestinians, might prove to be a bit unruly, particularly if Hugo expressed his views on the need for and importance of a consensual Israeli-Palestinian two-state solution. Without a consensual solution, Hugo believed any meaningful thoughts of pursuing a path to world peace could never occur.

In his speech, Hugo wisely decided not to venture into his views concerning who he thought owns what and where in the region. Rather, his message was pure and simple: peace will never be accomplished worldwide without compromise to territorial differences by the essential parties. And he promised if elected he would be a driving force behind a consensual agreement between the Palestinians and Israelis. He spoke at length on the reasons why the World needs a consensual solution. In a lecturing style, he told the audience that acceptance of religious differences by all spiritual groups would require a cultural change if there is ever to be any hope for global peace.

Hugo then changed topics. He spoke at length on the sudden influx of illegal immigrants entering the United States at our southern border. He referenced New York City as an example of areas in our country feeling the impact of the existing lax policy on immigration. He said our immigration policy needs fixing—and needs fixing right away. He said he had a plan to amend our immigration policies to provide tighter controls over all immigrants, to prohibit the entry of all immigrants not legally authorized to be here, and to deport all illegal immigrants within our borders.

Hugo briefly touched on his plan to put more money into the pockets of lower-income earners so that more citizens could share in the American Dream.

Hugo ended his speech about 9:20 p.m. to boisterous, scattered partisan shouts, cheers, and jeers—an expected crowd reaction. Hugo had wanted to remain and mingle among the crowd, but his campaign assistants thought otherwise and hustled Hugo and Louise through a side exit of the Garden into the rear of the second of two black stretch limousines awaiting his departure. Hugo's driver had instructions to drive Hugo and Louise directly to their home in Essex, Connecticut.

Hugo had confidence that their driver, Zack, would get them home safely. After all, Zack was one of the owners of Zack's Limo Services, and it was Zack who had driven Hugo and Louise to the Garden earlier that evening.

Shortly after the limos departed from the Garden area, Hugo disengaged his seat belt, reached over and grabbed a mini bottle of Chardonnay, which had been chilling in the limo's mini-bar, poured the entire contents into a glass intended for drinking white wine, and then handed Louise the glass. He then mixed and treated himself to his favorite mood-altering beverage—a hefty-sized dirty vodka martini, made with two mini-bottles of vodka and a dash of olive juice, both poured over an olive and one ice cube in a rock glass. Hugo was glad the speech was over. He was stressed and tired.

Bumper to bumper, the limo Hugo was in zigzagged through a route along the Cross Bronx Expressway to I-95 in lower Westchester

County, across the New York state line into Greenwich, Connecticut, and then continuing along I-95 through Stamford, Bridgeport, and Milford. The first limo stopped in Stamford, where the campaign staff planned to spend the night. The traffic had been relatively light in Connecticut until reaching the Campbell Avenue section of West Haven.

Hugo had fallen asleep by the time the limo reached the Connecticut border. When nearing West Haven, Louise noticed Hugo was still asleep, hardly breathing, and his face had turned bluish gray. Then suddenly Hugo's head jerked up and he tried to vomit, but couldn't. He started choking, his body began convulsing uncontrollably, and he appeared in a total daze. Louise screamed at him, "Hugo, wake up! Wake up! What's happening?"

Louise was panicking and yelled to Zack, "Pull the car over right now! Something's wrong with Hugo. He won't wake up."

Zack pulled off I-95 onto an exit ramp near New Haven Boulevard. He leaped out of the limo, opened the rear door, and applied a Heimlich maneuver, which didn't help. Then he felt Hugo's pulse, looked at Louise with a worried look, and said, "I'm calling 911 immediately!"

An emergency medical vehicle arrived within minutes. The medical team assessed Hugo and attempted to jolt his breathing mechanisms to revitalize his breathing essentials. They then informed Louise and Zack they had to rush Hugo to nearby Yale-New Haven Hospital. Shortly after Hugo was admitted into the Emergency Room, he was pronounced dead due to an apparent heart attack. A coroner's report was to follow within three days.

The coroner's report included evidence that a trace of cyanide was identified in Hugo's blood. The limo Hugo and Louise were in had never been considered a crime scene until well after the limo had been thoroughly cleaned in preparation for use by other customers.

Hugo McCormick

CHAPTER 2

Looking Back

★ ★ ★

Hugo McCormick, an Independent Party congressman from Congressional District 7 in Connecticut, waited until the House was on a three-week break before he announced his decision not to pursue a third term. By waiting, he hoped to escape the typical flow of commendatory oratory the House normally bestows on its retiring brothers and sisters. Several multi-term House members were known to specialize in spurning ritualistic sentiment on departing members, often causing some departing colleagues to have a fleeting moment or two regretting their decision to leave such "wonderful" friends.

Congressman McCormick had a canny eye and ear for shallow oratory wrapped up in blarney, and certainly had no thoughts of yielding to last minute nostalgia to remain in the legislative environment. He was an honest man, intelligent, transparent, and ethical. On matters he deemed important, Hugo passionately expressed his thoughts and beliefs—regardless of political ramifications. He was a politician for the people, not seeking personal aggrandizement but finding satisfaction in thinking he was doing a good job in representing the voters who elected him. He voted with his beliefs and feelings, refusing to play partisan political games that might have better served him if he were seeking positions of power within Congress. But he wasn't.

He found political life frustrating as it seemed to him that few in the House sought his thoughts or vote on important legislation. He could not recall one meaningful legislative accomplishment attributed to him during his two terms. So Hugo had many political reasons not to seek another term. One nonpolitical reason not then known by his colleagues and Washington acquaintances was that his two terms in office contributed to a stressful relationship between Hugo and his then wife, Maureen, ultimately resulting in a consensual divorce shortly after Hugo left office.

In his pre-political days, Hugo was a partner for twenty-three years in a small law firm in West Haven, Connecticut. He and Maureen were high school sweethearts, who grew up in West Haven, graduated from West Haven High School, married in the First Congregational Church in West Haven, and raised two daughters while living in a house they purchased on Ocean Avenue in West Haven. Few would dispute that Hugo and his family were blue-blood Westies.

During his years of practicing law, Hugo preferred not to become active in local politics nor was he affiliated with a political party. He did enjoy close associations with many who were involved in politics, including his two law partners who represented the City of West Haven in several capacities. But he distanced himself from all local party affiliations, preferring to be free from political pressures while pursuing other legal-related interests. He lectured on Constitutional Law at the University of New Haven and University of Connecticut School of Law and was active as a long-time member and once chairman of the Constitutional Law Committee of the Connecticut Bar Association.

It was not until a group of concerned voters from the West Haven, Woodbridge, and Orange areas, unhappy with the representation then being provided by Chester Bowen, an aging nine-term congressman from the 7th District, persuaded Hugo to oppose Congressman Bowen for the 7th District's House seat. Congressman Bowen, a lifetime Democrat and member of the old establishment, was accustomed to running unopposed. But he was old, a bit senile, and had lost touch with the voters he represented.

In January 2002, shortly after the Democratic Party again nominated Congressman Bowen to run for another term, Hugo was invited to attend a meeting of the Independent Party, the purpose being to discuss a possible candidate to oppose Congressman Bowen. Hugo attended the meeting with no thoughts of being that candidate. In fact, if he had known that the party members invited him to evaluate his credentials and appetite for running, he would not have attended. But, Hugo was not aware of what was in the minds of others attending the meeting. After discussing a short list of possible candidates and deliberating till the late hours, the members ultimately and almost unanimously decided on one candidate, Hugo McCormick. Not without considerable thought, Hugo accepted the party's nomination.

Hugo knew Congressman Bowen well. He called him Chester. Although Chester was considerably older, Hugo shared a drink or two with the Congressman, as both were more than rare patrons of a local sports bar in West Haven. Nevertheless, Hugo thought Chester was well beyond his worth in Congress, and that he could do a much better job. So, though the political odds were against him as an Independent, Hugo became a genuine *grass roots* candidate. He ran a clean and honest campaign, focusing on issues rather than personal attacks, legislation rather than political favors, and he held Town Hall sessions with voters to fully understand their desires and expectations. The November election resulted in a landslide victory for Hugo, and he was off to Washington in January 2003.

Hugo received a real lesson in partisan politics while in Washington. He witnessed firsthand that the two major political parties were so polarized that chess matches among party leaders bogged down important legislation on the table for consideration. He witnessed firsthand a government that could no longer function efficiently in the manner conceived by our ancestors, as well as a political system that was starving to be overhauled.

He observed that too many of his new colleagues were more concerned with their own personal images and political goals, than focusing on the campaign promises made to become elected. It didn't take Hugo long to realize that as an Independent with no political influence, he was as important to congressional action as a grain of sand is to a beach renourishment program.

When Hugo left Washington four years later, he was embarrassed with what little he had accomplished. Not because he didn't put forth the effort, but because the system just didn't allow him to advance legislation he believed Congress should enact.

After leaving Washington, Hugo decided against returning to his law practice in West Haven, in part because he was embarrassed he had accomplished very little of what he promised he would do if elected. But primarily because he found out his wife, Maureen, had been having an affair with one of his law partners during his last two years as a congressman. Hugo and Maureen had a consensual divorce, which became final in 2007.

Rather than practice law, Hugo was offered an opportunity by an old friend, Jack Lambert, to author weekly politically oriented editorials for Jack's paper, *The Hartford Globe*. No, the pay would not be great, and he would have to meet publication guidelines, but being an editorialist would give him the opportunity to be a voice in the same political venue that had ignored him for four years. Hugo summed up his accomplishments in Washington with one sentence: "Nobody really gave a damn what he had to say."

"Yes," said Hugo to Jack upon accepting the position offered, "but only if you let me be my own man. I'll guarantee your paper will have a reputation for having at least one reputable editorialist."

Professor Crum

CHAPTER 3

Professor Crum's Political Science Class
9/19/2023

★ ★ ★

It was a few minutes before 10 and Professor Eric Crum already was in his seat at the center of a large, round conference table in a small classroom. While the other seats around the table were being filled with students, Professor Crum fiddled with his laptop to locate the spreadsheet that contained the names and academic backgrounds of the fifteen students who would constitute his class for the semester.

Professor Crum had an academic and achievement record which began in the early 1970s when he graduated Magna Cum Laude from Princeton University. He had a twenty-seven-year civil service record that included several high-level federal administrative appointments, including four years as United States Ambassador to Pakistan. While an adjunct professor of Political Science at Yale University, he authored two books relating to the role of the United States in activities beyond its borders—both books making the *New York Times* Best Sellers List. Five years ago, he was appointed to the position of professor and head of the Political Science Department at Duke University. He considered retiring more than once, but thought he still had more to offer before he packed it in.

"Good morning. I'm Eric Crum. You can call me Doctor Crum or Professor Crum. I prefer the latter. I'll be your instructor for this course. Unless you're in the wrong classroom, you should all be seniors or graduate students who chose to take this advanced course on political science. This is a six-week crash course, so we have lots to cover in very little time. Classes will begin sharply at ten and end at 11:30. We'll be covering in a philosophical and pragmatic manner the political environment as it exists in the United States today, with particular emphasis on political parties, the election process, public opinion, voters and voting, how our government operates, and whatever else you feel needs to be discussed to better understand the current political environment here in the United States.

"I have chosen a round conference table setting as this course will have no value without your participation. Whatever your political thoughts and beliefs now are, whether you know it or not, several of you will be among those who soon will be influencing and shaping decisions in our country and in countries abroad. This is not a lecture course, so don't expect me to sit here and express my views on the political environment or how it will change in the future. Why not? Simply because I don't know what path our country will take in future years. I hope this course better prepares you for the future decisions each of you will have to make as you proceed along the paths you'll soon choose on your journey through life. Any questions so far?"

Hearing none, Professor Crum continued. "The purpose of the course is to encourage and provoke the exchange of thoughts and views on the political, social, and economic issues important to you, me, the United States, and all countries beyond our borders—NO limitations on what you want to discuss. Say what you think and believe. What seems important to any one of you might not be as important to others in this class and vice versa.

"I have some thoughts on how this can be most beneficial. But your input is essential. Anyone have any suggestions on making this course meaningful and thought-provoking?"

After a brief silence, another voice was heard. "Professor Crum, I don't want to sound negative, but I hope this course is more than a bunch of us sitting around arguing partisan politics. I'd rather do that in a bar-room setting."

"Fair comment," Professor Crum responded. "What's your name?"

"Larry David. I didn't mean to be critical, but I took this course because I've been told you'd make us think."

"Sure hope you're not disappointed, Larry. I'll do my part. Anyone else like to comment?"

Hearing none, Professor Crum continued, "Fine. Here's the plan. We will break early today. But I want each of you to prepare and give me a brief one-page resume telling me who you are and why you're taking this course. Be honest and discreet, not too personal.

"Unless you request otherwise, I plan to make your resume available to the others in this course. At a minimum, your resume should include your name, address, brief family background, political affiliation, if any, and any involvement you've had in politics or with a political party. This will help us get to know each other so that we will have a better understanding of viewpoints on the topics and issues we'll be discussing.

"In addition, and on a separate piece of paper, I'd like each of you to set forth and prioritize the six most important issues you believe need to be addressed by our next president—and why. Please have this information in my office no later than next Monday. See you next Tuesday."

CHAPTER 4

Tike's Diner – Durham, NC

Tike's Diner was located next to the Exxon gas station across the highway from Duke's East Campus. The diner was not a place where one goes for fine dining, but rather an after-class hangout for Duke students to enjoy a late afternoon or early evening hot dog or grilled cheese with chips while sipping a can or two of the least expensive beverage sold in the state, National Bohemian. This beer had a reputation among Dukies as the only beer sold in a can where the foam remains hidden on the bottom.

The diner was open daily from 6 a.m. to 9 p.m. At any time during the day, local customers could buy a breakfast of two eggs any style, bacon or country ham, grits, juice, coffee, and toast for just $4.75. Lunch at the diner was limited to basic sandwiches. Tike's had the best grilled cheese and tomato with mayonnaise sandwich in town.

Justin Alibi, a senior at Duke, worked part-time as assistant manager at Tike's. He had been working there for a little more than two years, often working the 4 p.m. to 9 p.m. shift. Tike, owner of the diner, thought Justin to be an honest and reliable young man, and trusted him to close the diner when he left early. Tuesday afternoons and evenings typically were slow, and that's why Tuesdays were Tike's day off. Justin would let the other employees leave early on Tuesday evenings, and he'd stick around after closing to prepare the diner for opening the following morning.

Justin was one of the fifteen students in Professor Crum's Fall Political Science class.

CHAPTER 5

Professor Crum's 2nd Class
9/26/2023

The large, round, antique-looking clock on the wall said 10 a.m. The professor was settled into his chair at the conference table sorting through student papers left for him the day before. He was impressed with the varied backgrounds and accomplishments of the students who would be with him for the semester. "I made copies of each of your resumes. Those interested can pick up copies after class. Anyone have a problem with that?"

Seeing no objections, Professor Crum proceeded to give each student a three by four inch free-standing cardboard placard on which their name was inexpensively printed, asking that the placards be placed in front of them at the beginning of each session.

"Basil Kantor. New Hampshire. Hmmm … you're not related to Professor Dante Kantor at Dartmouth?"

"Yes, sir," said a voice two seats from the professor's right side. "That's my grandfather."

"Good to have you with us, Basil. I shouldn't tell you this, but your grandfather and I did a few things we probably shouldn't have while classmates at Princeton."

"Yes, he told me about his days at Princeton, Professor. I promise to keep them to myself—that is unless I'm not satisfied with my grade."

The professor responded by nodding his head, doing so with a confidence that his old college pal, Dante, certainly wouldn't mention to his grandson that he and Dante were almost booted out of Princeton their sophomore year when the campus police, late one night, walked in on him, Dante, and a few others, surrounded by a pile of empty beer cans, playing poker in Dante's dorm room. The police reported the incident to Princeton's Student Conduct Council (SCC), asserting Dante and Professor Crum not only violated the school's drinking regulations, but also the two appeared to be *three sheets to the wind.* Fortunately, the president of SCC, a fraternity brother of Dante, neglected to put the campus drinking violation on the SCC agenda of disciplinary matters to be addressed.

"Let's get started," said the professor. "Zada, I'll start by picking on you. I don't recall seeing your list of important items the next president should address."

Zada Nogah was seated across the conference table from Professor Crum. Her face turned from a light tan to a reddish-brown color. A second-generation Iranian, Zada appeared embarrassed by her being the first to be called on the carpet. A tall, sleek, attractive, and flirtatious girl with long-streaming auburn hair, Zada gave the appearance of being shy and self-conscious. She was anything but that.

Her dress alone revealed she was *Americanized*—she wore designer jeans, a black knit, collarless sweater-shirt, and well-worn tan flip-flops. She was Muslim, but not orthodox. She lived with her parents, both Iranians with college backgrounds, who had moved to the United States in 2007. Her father owned several convenience stores with attached gas stations in the West Palm Beach, Florida area.

"Sorry, I didn't forget my list, Professor. I have an excuse, but I'm sure you don't want to hear it. If it's OK, I'll hand in my list by the end of today. Promise."

"No need to now, Zada. I'm sure you had a good excuse. But tell us, in your view, what should be the two most critical issues the next president should address?"

Zada wasn't born yesterday. She saw this coming—and was prepared. She stared at the professor for a moment, and then responded: "Peace in the Mideast, and the widespread poverty that exists throughout the world. What could be more important to the president than these problems?"

"Can't argue with you," responded the professor. "Anyone differ with Zada?"

"Those are lofty thoughts, Zada," said Ryan McPherson, a short, stocky red-headed Irish American and son of a former speechwriter for George W. Bush in the early 2000s. Ryan, seated next to Zada, then added, "But let's be realistic. Before the president takes on worldly issues, he or she needs to clean up how our own government operates. It's a mess. Partisan politics is crippling Congress. The next president needs to focus his attention on mending the fences between the political parties so that Congress will be able to execute its responsibilities on critical national and international matters."

"What do you mean, Ryan? Be more specific," queried the professor.

"Well, look at the way our government operates. It's a mess—a huge, complex, antiquated machine that needs to be completely overhauled. The people we continually elect to office, once in office, become too polarized, too partisan, so bent on getting re-elected that regardless of which party is in power, very little of substance gets accomplished. Or so it seems. World peace, hunger, whatever—I agree with Zada that these areas are, pardon the expression, starving for solutions.

"But the president is powerless to bring about any meaningful changes to such worldly needs without help from both aisles of Congress. We need a government which will respond more effectively to important demands, one that will work in harmony to achieve solutions to meaningful matters. Our legislative system might be too far gone. I think it needs better management and policies to better serve the needs of our country."

"You seem energized, Ryan," remarked the professor. "Is that the only thing on which the next president should focus?"

"Hardly! You got me going," said Ryan. "What about immigration, energy resources, water supply, global warming, or drugs and crime? Our politicians are so partisan that meaningful action on anything controversial is like watching an ant swallow an elephant. Can you recall the last time our legislators seriously discussed controversial legislation without partisan politics getting in the way of responsible action?"

Liz Reicher raised her hand, prompting the professor to say, "Yes, Liz. You have something to add?"

Liz, who never experienced poverty or hard work in her life, was born and raised in Rye, New York. Her parents, both born in the US, were Jewish and so was she. Her father was one of the principal owners of a large real estate investment firm, with offices in New York City, Chicago, and Stamford, Connecticut. Like most other students in the Professor's classes, Liz was no shrinking violet. Her hazel brown eyes, long walnut-brown hair, slightly pointed nose, gloating smile, and natural frown produced an appearance of an erudite, sophisticated snob, which of course, she said she wasn't—but those who knew her said she was. When she wore her dark brown, horn-rimmed glasses, her friends fittingly referred to her as *the wise old owl*. Like her father, she was a hawk on Mideast strategies, and a strong advocate of the rights of the Israeli people to defend and preserve their homeland. Her father assisted Joe Lieberman in 2006 in his run for re-election to the US Senate in Connecticut.

"What could be more important to us now than our own security?" said Liz, hesitant to express her views on the Israeli-Palestinian conflict. "We are being overwhelmed at our borders, particularly our southern border, by immigrants with all sorts of backgrounds, many who soon will pose a threat to our way of life as feeders to militant terrorist groups. Why does our administration stubbornly resist working together to enact legislation which will thwart what is becoming a serious threat to our way of life? I understand immigrants who are not even citizens recently have been granted voting rights in several states, including New York and Vermont."

"What are your thoughts, Enrique? Or is it Henry?"

"I'm Henry here in the States, but in my country I'm Enrique. You want my thoughts on the Arab-Israeli war or world-wide peace?"

"Whatever you want to comment on," said the professor.

Henry, a graduate student from Spain, looked like a Spaniard should, ate Spanish food, practiced Spanish customs, yet spoke English as well as most Englishmen, choosing each word carefully. He was making his first visit to the States, hoping this class would be a forum which would give him a better understanding of America's goals and objectives as arguably the *leader of the free world.*

"I don't understand American politics," Henry began. "You elect a president to lead your people, yet how much authority does he really have over the important issues that need government action? He must work with members of Congress to pass needed legislation, yet the members of Congress are so polarized, so partisan that passing any kind of meaningful legislation is a struggle. If this is the way a democratic government works, maybe the concept shouldn't be exported to other countries."

"Guess you're not too impressed with the way our country operates are you, Henry? You think a dictatorship would be better for our country?" said the professor, as though baiting a response.

"I don't know," said Henry, "Maybe. That's why I came here to Duke—to better understand how a democracy functions."

"Henry makes a good point," the professor said to the group. "Maybe we should be taking a good look at how our government operates. It had been working reasonably well for years, but is it broken now? Can it be repaired or fixed? And how? The 2024 presidential election is less than a year away. Maybe we should explore what the candidates running for the presidency think about the important issues the next president will need to address. We'll do that next Tuesday."

The classroom slowly emptied, except for Justin Alibi. Professor Crum remained at the table jotting down a few notes. Justin lagged behind, intending to speak to the professor about something bothering him. However, he had second thoughts, and left saying nothing.

CHAPTER 6

Abdul's House, Maryland
9/29/2023

★ ★ ★

The house at the end of the cul-de-sac on Bushnell Court in Randallstown, Maryland, was owned by Abdul Kadir and his wife, Kristina. Abdul, who came to the States from Saudi Arabia eight years ago, had been a US citizen since he turned 28 in 2020. He was the owner of a Taco Bell franchise located in Baltimore. Kristina, a stout person of German stock, was born and raised in a small town in Missouri. They met when both were applying for citizenship in 2019 and married in 2020. Shortly after they married, they purchased the home in which they now live, a modest seven-room house with three bedrooms and baths and a large kitchen. They had no children or pets.

"Anyone else coming?" asked Jam, a twenty-nine-year-old Iranian whose real first name was Jammat. Jam, employed as a longshoreman at the Baltimore docks, was the tacit leader of a radical Islamic cell group which had been holding meetings at Abdul's house every other Friday for the past two years.

"Only Kareem and a friend he is bringing," said Abdul. "I don't know much about the friend, but Kareem said we should talk to him—and he can be trusted. We shall see. His name is Justin."

At 8:10 p.m., a black Lexus 330 SUV flashing its high beams three times pulled into the driveway. Though not a clandestine signal, it was adequate for the informal gathering. Kareem and Justin exited the car and after a courteous three knock rap, entered the house through the back door of the kitchen. "Sorry we're late." said Kareem. "This is Justin, a good man. He's from our North Carolina region. Professor Ibala thinks he could help us."

Cautiously, Justin looked around and then nodded to the others in the kitchen. He was hesitant to say anything of substance as he knew little about those in the room. It didn't take long for Justin to realize the people he would soon meet were more than an aimless cell group. They appeared to be mature, serious, no-nonsense persons—gathering for a purpose.

"I thought there would be more people here. Is this *The Group*?" asked Justin, not knowing what else to say.

"Not everyone," answered Jam. "You'll meet others on a need-to-know basis."

Jam reminded everyone there that no recordings or notes are to be kept of their meetings. He didn't feel he had to remind everyone that alcohol, guns, drugs, or explosive devices also were not to be brought to the meetings.

After polite introductory chatter, *The Group* sat around an oval-shaped glass-top breakfast table with Jam leading the discussion, careful not to mention the names of others in the cell network. He relayed the concern from the top that somewhere within the network information is being leaked to federal sources, and that plans for the event scheduled for July 4th have been put on hold.

Justin inquired about the Fourth of July plan, but Jam said he would prefer not to talk of details as they might be aborted. He talked about the significant growth of Jihadism here in the States and the need to be watchful for infiltrators. They must keep reminding each other, *"The time for Jihad is now."*

Nothing of substance was planned that night, but Jam ended the session with the comment, "If plans for July 4th are a go, one of the mother cells will be expecting us to become involved." He suggested members of *The Group* continue blending in with everyday living as the Feds are keeping close tabs on what it calls freedom fighters and cell groups. He warned the others that the Feds are profiling Islamic groups and followers, particularly in major cities near airports and military establishments.

The meeting lasted until 10:30, the time Kristina was expected to return from a visit with her mother. At Abdul's suggestion, Kristina made the visit to see her mother every other Friday at the same time.

CHAPTER 7

Professor Crum's 3rd Class
10/3/2023

★ ★ ★

Professor Crum was five minutes early for his class. He took pride in being punctual. His class started at 10 sharp. He let his students know they could rely on his being there at 10 a.m., so he expected them to be in their seats at the same time. According to Professor Crum, being punctual was an act of discipline, of courtesy, and of respect. Rarely were his students late to his classes.

When the large wall clock said 10 a.m., Professor Crum acknowledged the students with a roaming glance and then said, "OK, let's begin where we left off last Tuesday. Let's start with you, Jon. Who among the presidential candidates do you think should be elected our next president?"

Jon Chen, a Vietnam exchange student, son of parents who both graduated from Yale Medical School and now are physicians in Vietnam, looked at Professor Crum and wondered why he was being asked this question. After all, he was not a US citizen, he had no intention to remain in the United States after graduate school, and he didn't pay too much attention to the candidates running for the presidency. Therefore, he didn't really care about the outcome of the election. He was hoping to sit and listen, expecting to gain an understanding from Professor Crum and his class members of how the US Government functions. Sensing his attitude, Professor Crum, unwilling to accept sideline students, nudged Jon's participation.

With a nonchalant expression on his face, Jon responded, "There are so many candidates seeking the presidency. I haven't a clue as to who is best qualified. But it appears that voters will have to choose between Biden and Trump. This seems like another presidential year when voters will be stuck with electing a president who is neither liked nor respected. Your election process should produce better nominees."

"Baloney!" shouted Ted Stuart after listening to Jon's *I don't care* response.

"You'd better explain yourself, Ted. What's wrong with Jon suggesting alternatives to Biden and Trump?"

"He hasn't mentioned alternatives," said Ted, "nor has he mentioned the qualities of a candidate he might support. I do agree that a Biden versus Trump matchup offers little choice. But we must look beyond Biden and Trump to find a person who will be respected by all political parties here in the States and by the leaders of countries around the world. We need someone capable of tearing down the steel wall between the political parties which is hampering legislative action, like passing the general federal budget or adopting effective controls to prevent illegal immigrants from entering our country."

Professor Crum could see several students nodding in agreement with Ted's comments, so he urged him to continue. "So, Ted, regardless of what you think of Trump or Biden, they might just be the nominees in the next presidential election. If so, who would be your choice?"

Ted hadn't been prepared to compare the qualifications of either. But this didn't stop him from expressing his views. "From what I read in the papers and heard on TV, Joe Biden is not only too old to handle the pressures of another term, but his poll numbers indicate people are dissatisfied with how he has been handling the economy and immigration. Internationally, he projects an image of weakness in the eyes of the leaders of foreign countries by the manner in which we withdrew our troops from Iraq, our lack of willingness to fully support Ukraine's efforts to fend off Russia's attempt for territorial gains, our reluctance to act against Iran for attacks against our troops by puppets of Iran, and the weak responses to both North Korea and China rattling their weapons of war.

"As for Donald Trump, his bullying approach to solving world problems is not popular with many voters. I think Trump might be running to seek retribution against those who are critical of him, or maybe to avoid the several criminal charges against him. It has been reported that he has said if elected he will pursue criminal charges against many who have opposed him, including Joe Biden. Trump has a reputation for being impulsive, often motivated by his own feelings and concerns, rather than those of the country. He can do no wrong— or so he thinks."

"Thanks, Ted, for not burying your thoughts. No doubt you're a person *who says it like you see it.* Anyone else have thoughts on who our next president should be? What about you, Crystal?"

Crystal Brown, a short, athletic-looking girl, was the only black person in the class. At the high school she attended in Philadelphia, she was vice president of her class, a member of the National Honor Society, captain of the girls' softball team, president of the school's debating teams, and participated in numerous non-scholastic activities, including president of Philadelphia's Youth Democratic Society. Crystal, a full scholarship recipient at Duke, is a member of Duke's debating team, and currently is president of Duke's Gay-Lesbian Society.

Crystal had been patiently waiting to share her thoughts. "You probably think I disagree with Ted, but I don't. Who would I prefer to be the next president? None of the above. That's right—the probable nominees are Biden and Trump, and neither deserve to be elected president next November."

Before Professor Crum could ask Crystal to explain her reasoning, Adam Wiehl, sitting next to Crystal, clapped his hands and said, "Ain't that the truth! I also would not vote for either Biden or Trump or any of the other candidates who might be running."

After several others in the class joined in to express similar thoughts and feelings, Professor Crum pounded his fist on the desk and yelled, "Whoa! It's going to be difficult to discuss the presidential election if none of you like any of the choices. Let's have a show of hands. Who would vote for either Joe Biden or Donald Trump to be the next president?" No hands were raised.

"No surprise. Who might vote for any of the other possible candidates?"

Zada was the only student who raised her hand. "I might vote for Chris Christie," said Zada. "He's not in the best physical shape, a bit hefty around the middle, but he's a tough, transparent, no-nonsense communicator, and a proven administrator who gets things done. I like him—at least compared to the other choices."

Hearing no other voices, Professor Crum asked Sam Austin if he'd care to share his thoughts. Sam lived with his parents in Winter

Sam Austin

Springs, Florida, when he's not in school. He's a political science major with flashes of interest in entering politics. "I know what my father would want. He'd like Barack Obama to run again. But I'm not my father. I agree with the others. I might consider voting for Senator Manchin, but he's not running—yet. I understand he's toying with the thought of running as nominee of the recently established No Labels Party. But he's 76 now and has expressed thoughts of completely retiring from politics. I'd even consider voting for Mitt Romney as he has announced he won't be seeking reelection to the Senate. However, he's not young either."

"So, you wouldn't vote for any of the announced Democrat or Republican candidates either?" questioned Professor Crum.

"I guess that's what I'm saying," responded Sam.

"So where do we go from here?" inquired Professor Crum, as he sat back in his chair, rolled his eyes, extended his arms in front of him with palms of hands facing upwards, as though he was trying to catch something falling from above—hoping and expecting to ignite spirited reactions from his students.

He wanted the class to orchestrate the next move. That was Professor Crum's style. He considered he would be the one furnishing the stimulus, channeling his students into a thought-provoked environment where the students would *think outside the box*. It took the professor a few sessions to set the stage, but now he was ready to see where the class would take him.

"You know, Professor Crum," said Ryan, "It's still early in the election cycle. It's not too late for someone with better credentials and leadership qualities to run for the presidency. Unfortunately, both major parties appear to already have made their nominee choices."

"So, Ryan, what are you saying?" asked Professor Crum. "Should we just let the election process play out and accept the fact that the Democratic and Republican parties will be limiting your choice to persons you feel would not be good presidents?"

"'I probably won't vote," said Ryan. "Whatever happens, happens. Far too many persons are like me and won't bother voting, primarily because they think none of the nominees have convinced us they were worthy of being president."

"So, you throw up your hands,' said Professor Crum. "Not what I wanted to hear."

"I have a thought," said Liz. "It's early October. There's still over a year until the election. If none of us like the slate of persons being considered for the presidency, why not mold our own candidate—fictitious, albeit, but someone who would possess the qualifications we think a candidate should have to earn our votes. What do you think of that, Professor Crum? Let's add some meat to this course!"

The professor scratched his head while looking at Liz, hoping she wouldn't detect the glitter in his eye or his attempt to restrain his satisfaction that someone finally proposed a course of action he would have mandated, had it not been proposed.

"You want meat,' said Professor Crum. "I'll give you more than you'll be able to eat. Let's say you not only identify the qualifications you'd like to see in our next president, but you find an actual person who possesses most, if not all, those qualifications. Perhaps someone who is not a career politician, but is someone with the leadership skills, desired temperament, and knowledgeable in matters important to our country.

"And why stop there? Let's assume you can identify someone whom you feel would make a good president. What would you do to encourage him or her to run for the presidency? Now that's meat! Not only is that meat, but identifying a candidate and planning a path to the presidency for this candidate is your class project for this course."

Excitement and tacit approval could be seen on the faces of all the students, except Jon. Class projects such as the one just outlined by the professor were the reason students took Professor Crum's course. He demanded participation—yes. And one never knew exactly what to expect.

But Jon had reservations about such a project. "Hogwash!" he yelled. "How could all of us agree on an ideal candidate? Liz and I probably couldn't agree on what today's date is."

"Ah, Jon, but that's where the real world kicks in," countered the professor. "Of course, most of you will have different views on governing matters, as well you should have. You don't have the same cultural background. Many of you come from countries with political and social beliefs quite different from those in the United States. All of you have learned what you know and believe from those who have been part of your growth experience. So, as a group, you won't agree on everything. But to exist in this world, you need to agree or at least compromise on some things. For those matters of disagreement, sort out what's good or not good for those who will be affected, and then make compromises.

"I applaud this class. I think you selected a worthwhile project to pursue," stated the professor.

CHAPTER 8

The Chalkboard
10/10/2023

★ ★ ★

The conference room had a slide-down chalkboard centered against the wall within easy view of the class members with slight spinning or tilting of their chairs. Professor Crum was writing on the board as the students were being seated. He wrote the last name of each student in two columns before he returned to his chair.

"Ready for some meat?" Professor Crum rhetorically asked. "Let's call the candidate we will be seeking to identify as 'X'. We're not ready to identify X today, but, in order to reach common ground on what we'd like to see in our choice of a president, let's start by naming six or seven key issues that will serve as the nucleus of a proposed platform for X. We need serious and realistic input. That's where you come in.

"I wrote each of your names on the chalkboard. Now I would like each of you to jot down next to your name the most important area of concern you think X should address if he were to become president. OK, Zada. Let's start with you. Then after Zada, we'll proceed around the table clockwise. Adam, you're next. Any questions?"

"What if I agree with Zada on what she puts down?" said Adam. "Then what?"

"I should have been clearer," responded Professor Crum. "Don't put down an issue already selected by someone else. We want to end up with fifteen different concerns. Basil, since you're the last person to write down a concern, you might find it difficult to name one. But those are the breaks. We can do this."

Zada confidently strutted to the board and wrote beside her name, *World Peace*. Adam followed with *Immigration and Illegal Immigrants*. One by one the list grew: *Israeli—Palestinian Crisis*; *Health Care*; *Crime in Our Cities*; *World Hunger*; *Space Program*; *Interplanetary Exploration*; *Artificial Intelligence*; *Media Reporting*; *Abortion Rights*; *Partisan Politics*; *Environment*; *Hate Crimes*; and *Gross Income Disparity.*

"Quite an impressive list," stated Professor Crum. "And I see nobody mentioned entitlements, welfare programs, tax reform, the budget, and our economy. Who said Gross Income Disparity?"

"I did," said Basil.

"Could you elaborate?" asked Professor Crum.

"That wasn't my number one concern," said Basil. But here in the United States and abroad, we are experiencing social and economic problems substantially attributable to the disparity in income levels of the haves and have-nots. I identify with most capitalistic principles, but it's clear that many Americans earn poverty-level incomes and thus are not able to share in the American Dream. I think when income slots a person into an environment of poverty, for whatever reason, stealing and dealing in drug-related activities to supplement income is not a challenging leap."

"Sounds like you'd like the next president to push for some form of income controls," said Professor Crum.

"No, no, not that!" Basil emphatically responded. "I haven't really thought this through, but I'm more concerned with the typical hard-working person who works eight to five in a factory, office, or wherever. This person might be a high school graduate or dropout—doesn't matter. Might even be a college graduate. I'm talking about the people who work hard at low-paying jobs to support a spouse and family on an income, say, under $50,000. Even with annual cost of living increases, this family continually struggles to meet their everyday living expenses. Families in this income range typically can't afford a house, new car, or go to a major league ball game—and probably never will. For many, the only hope to climb beyond near poverty level is to become involved in illegal activities—or win the lottery. Where's the American Dream for them? Where's the incentive to continue working at a job where unemployment becomes a better option than working?"

"So what are you telling us, Basil?" asked Professor Crum, sensing that Basil had more to say.

"I'm not sure, Professor. But let's look at the other end of the income spectrum. Without diminishing the importance of rewarding those who genuinely deserve to be rewarded financially for their performances or accomplishments, far too many persons are rewarded with pay packages far beyond what's reasonable compensation for what they're doing. I'm not talking about those one-time pay packages to attract quality leaders and managers. I'm talking about annual incomes that go far beyond what a normal person should be rewarded for services performed."

"That's the way a capitalistic and free enterprise system operates, Basil," said Professor Crum. "It's been working that way for years. You want to change it now?"

"I don't want to change it entirely. I just think it should be modified so that our society will reward those who strive to lift themselves to a higher income level, but can't. If too many people can't lift themselves out of near poverty level, then we better watch out. Our capitalist way of life might come under attack, and we could experience more than creeping socialism. I wouldn't like that."

"Continue, I'm listening," said Professor Crum.

"In my view," said Basil, executive compensation for many has become a game of greed, a game where certain executives compete among others seeking to become among the elite in total compensation. Is this a fair apportionment of income? Excessive pay packages to high-level corporate executives are not even fair to shareholders, who, for the most part, have only superficial control over corporate pay. And what about the *golden parachutes* that often reward what seems to be unconscionable sums to executives who have performed poorly and have been asked to resign or retire?"

"Not just corporate executives," said Angus Subine, who until now, had managed to be a closet-case participant. Angus came from a family with lots of money, though by looking at him, one could conclude he owned only one set of clothes. His father, CEO of a major food distribution chain with worldwide recognition, recently was written up in the business section of *The Wall Street Journal* as one of the highest-paid corporate executives in the United States.

"What about professional jocks?" continued Angus. "Compare what your typical policeman, fireman, or teacher earns to the average salaries of baseball, football, or basketball players. Several of these players sign contracts for annual incomes of more than one hundred million dollars. For what—to hit a few baseballs into the grandstands, or throw or receive a few touchdown passes, or score 25 or 30 points a game? How about professional golfers or tennis players! Is a boxing championship title match worth fifty to one hundred million dollars to the winner? I think most corporate CEOs earn what they're paid, but how do you justify paying persons who are good at a sport to be paid such enormous amounts when there are so many *little guys* working long shifts only to tread water to keep from going under?"

"I agree with Angus," added Macy, another student in the class who had yet to express himself. What about those so-called rock stars, rappers, and other entertainers? I read recently in *Forbes Magazine* that in 2022, Genesis reportedly received about 220 million in gross income—and Sting grossed some 210 million. Ever heard of Bad Bunny? He's a Puerto Rican rapper who grossed 88 million in 2022. And today Taylor Swift is far and away the biggest earner—she's now a billionaire. I don't know what other performers make, but I wouldn't be surprised if Dolly Parton, Katy Perry, P Diddy, Madonna, and Rihanna each earned more than 200 million in 2023. Does anybody deserve to earn that much income in a year when there are so many workers in the United States who must clip coupons to make ends meet? What are they going to do with all that money, buy ten cars and four or five homes?"

Basil had not yet finished ranting about disproportionate incomes among certain members of our society. "Let's not let the lawyers off the hook either. Just last week I received a check which represented my share of a 330 million-dollar settlement in a class-action suit brought against Bank of America. My settlement check was for 72 cents. What did the lawyers receive? You bet—eighty-six million dollars plus expenses. And this lawsuit was considered a small class-action settlement case.

"According to my father, class-action lawyers make fortunes suing corporate giants on rather insignificant issues. Then, because of the enormous time and expense to litigate such cases, they negotiate a settlement with large corporate defendants for amounts that pay little to the class members who might have suffered a loss. It's a mockery of the legal system—all in the name of the lawyers protecting us poor consumers."

Intending to further fuel the discussion, Professor Crum asked "So what's the big deal? That's the way it is in a competitive society.

If you're good at something and you can make it pay off—well, go for it. Where's your entrepreneurial spirit?"

"You're putting us on, Professor," remonstrated Basil. "Certainly, I wouldn't want to discourage entrepreneurship, or motivation, or the desire to succeed. Maybe the government should exempt household net incomes of persons or families with annual net incomes of less than $100,000. That would immediately put more money in the pockets of low-income persons."

"True," agreed the professor, "but wouldn't the IRS see a substantial shortage of income?"

"Yes," responded Basil, "but changing the tax laws to increase taxes on excessive incomes would more than offset lost revenues from exempting income of those earning net income of less than $100,000."

"Anyone agree with Basil?" inquired Professor Crum. All but Justin and Henry raised their hands. "Congratulations, Basil. This will be one of the concerns to consider when searching for candidate X. What shall we label this concern?"

"Robin Hood Social Justice," mocked Henry with a smirk, expecting to get a rise out of Basil.

"How about *Income Justice?*" proposed Crystal, recognizing that the substance of income justice is more important than the label.

"*Income Justice* it is," agreed the professor.

The class then began rattling off other matters that should be part of X's platform. The entire class agreed that *World Peace* should be at the top of the list. Also considered important were *Immigration, Management and Control of Outer Space; Improving the Legislative Process;* and *The Character, Personality, and Leadership Capabilities of the Nominee.*

Professor Crum reviewed the following six areas the class agreed should constitute X's campaign platform: *World Peace; Income*

Justice; Character and Effective Leadership; U.S. Space Program; Immigration; and our Political System.

All fifteen categories on the chalkboard were ticked off and incorporated into one or more of the six vital areas of concern. According to Professor Crum, "The search for X would include his views on how he or she would address the issues on this proposed platform."

CHAPTER 9

Group Nabbed—
Randallstown, Maryland
10/15/2023

★ ★ ★

Early Sunday morning, Justin strolled over to the Duke Coffee Shop to purchase an expresso and the *Durham Daily News,* a local newspaper. He sat by himself, intending to read the paper while sipping his expresso. His eyes immediately were drawn to the headline of a lengthy article that appeared at the bottom of the first page and continued to the second page. The article was captioned: "Terrorist Plot Foiled." Justin read the following article in its entirety.

On Friday evening, October 6th, thirty FBI agents burst into a small, three-bedroom house on a quiet cul-de-sac in Randallstown, Maryland, a town on the outskirts of Baltimore, Maryland, and within an hour's drive to Washington, DC. Three persons in the house were arrested on charges of conspiracy to conduct terrorist activities. Two trained dogs sniffed out areas on the property, where the agents found a cache of automatic weapons, high-powered explosives, sophisticated surveillance equipment, and several short-range howitzers tucked away in a hidden compartment behind a cinderblock cellar foundation wall. The suspected terrorists had been under FBI surveillance for over a year.

The owner of the property, Abdul Kadir, an Iranian immigrant, had been identified on an FBI Suspects List as a terrorist cell activist. He moved to the States from Iran in 2015 and has been employed for the past three years as the manager of a Taco Bell franchise in Baltimore. Kadir lived on the property with his wife, Kristina. He had no prior criminal record. According to sources, when Kristina was made aware her husband was being arrested, she became hysterical, shouting at the arresting agents that her husband is a non-violent man and is being illegally profiled as a terrorist.

Apparently Kadir had been living a double life, appearing to be a model citizen, while allegedly also being involved with an organized anti-American terrorist group with a presence within the US. A spokesperson for the FBI said that it had learned from an informant that the cell group with which Kadir was affiliated was planning an event at which President Biden would be present, and that it had to act hastily to prevent whatever was planned. The raid produced very little other than to get a few reported terrorists off the street.

One of the persons arrested was Bella Arista, Abdul's niece. Apparently, Bella had been in the States for two years on a student visa, studying languages and art at the University of Maryland. She is twenty-three years old, single, and, according to the school's records, spoke four languages fluently, including English. Bella claimed she was merely visiting her uncle and didn't know why she should be arrested.

The third person arrested was Carlos Padua, a 55-year-old Baltimore resident who worked for the past five years at a shipyard in Baltimore's harbor. His background is being investigated.

Several other alleged cell members who were not present during the raid are being sought.

FBI sources said the cell group allegedly is tapped into an international network of Muslim extremists who had entered the US as illegal immigrants coming from Mexico over the border.

In a conversation taped by FBI agents, an unidentified voice said that the terrorist organization had been informed that the

US recently approved plans to ship more equipment, including missiles, to Israel, destined to be used to kill Muslims, and that it was time to act.

FBI sources said that the planned terrorist attack was revealed by a law enforcement informant.

CHAPTER 10

Attacking the Source
10/20/2023

Hugo McCormick more than lived up to Jack's expectations. For the past fifteen years, *No More Small Talk* gave national recognition to *The Hartford Globe*—and to Hugo. His opinion column, published weekly in *The Globe,* is syndicated to multiple, long-established, perceived liberal and conservative publications across the country.

Hugo enjoyed a reputation as a person who, with no apparent personal agenda, would say what he thought was best for the country and the world, regardless of how others thought about what he had to say. He did not mince words. He wore his heart on his sleeve, often venting dissatisfaction on congressional complacency in failing to take responsible legislative action on matters of national and international importance. As a former member of Congress, he knew firsthand how partisan politics and personal greed crippled Congressional legislative action. He admitted carrying a personal grudge against partisan voting in Congress ever since his voice was virtually ignored when he served in Congress.

But it could be heard now. Hundreds of letters and emails poured into Hugo's office daily from readers throughout the country, most encouraging him to keep pressing politicians to act on the problems they talked about in campaign speeches. His editorials were on topics most politicians seeking office preferred to duck.

During the past year, Hugo expressed his thoughts on such controversial topics as the struggle to find peace between the Israelis and Palestinians, rising tensions among the powerful nuclear-weaponized countries, immigration and how immigration policies are adversely influencing our way of life, gangs and crimes and how the two concerns are becoming inseparable, space and control of outer space, and most important, instilling in the minds of world leaders that world peace among all nations acting together is essential to preserving mankind on Earth.

Hugo, in his editorials, continually urged members of Congress to "work together in a non-partisan way. Limit the gridlock that impedes the purpose you've been sent to Washington." Occasionally Hugo would receive an email from a reader who thought his idealistic pontifications were mere Pollyanna editorial talking points, but most emails expressed general agreement with what Hugo had to say.

"I admit I don't have all the solutions or answers," said Hugo, "but proposing answers or solutions would be mere guesswork without meaningful dialogue. And I see my job as facilitating meaningful dialogue."

Hugo had few friends in Washington. Why should he? Certain members of Congress needed to be exposed for non-performance or malperformance on matters requiring immediate and responsible action. Hugo was able to expose those legislators he felt needed to be exposed.

Even Jack did not always agree with some of Hugo's opinions. But, heck, his paper was selling, he was making money, and Hugo and his column were responsible for much of the paper's popularity. So Jack exercised little editorial control over Hugo, knowing Hugo would give him a "heads up" on anything he proposed writing that might impact the reputation of Jack or his paper. That's why Hugo left a copy of his next Sunday's editorial on Jack's desk.

Jack smiled when he saw the heading: *Too Much Bias in Media Reporting*. Jack, who recently gave up smoking, leaned back in his chair, put an unlit cigarette into his mouth, and hoped he wouldn't soon be reading something that would make him cringe.

Jack founded his paper to make money—sure. But more importantly, he wanted his paper to have a reputation for reporting the facts. "I want fair, honest, balanced, non-partisan reporting," Jack repeatedly told his reporters. "I don't want any evidence of bias or prejudiced reporting. Your job as reporters is to report the facts as you see them—no pontificating!" Jack wanted opinions to be identified as such and found only on the editorial pages of the paper. And he wanted those who wrote opinions to identify who they were, and with what party they were affiliated, if any.

Jack finished reading Hugo's proposed article for Sunday, then put it face up in his outbox after he made the notation: "Great job, Hugo. I couldn't agree more!"

Proposed Article: Too Much Bias in Media Reporting

By

Hugo McCormick

Former Congressman from Connecticut and now
syndicated editorialist with *The Hartford Globe*.
Not affiliated with any political party or organization.

In light of the upcoming presidential election, I challenge reporters from the news media to alter their often biased style of reporting. I'm not referring to editorialists. They're not reporters. Editorialists do not report facts. They interpret the facts as they see them … and then write opinions. That's their job. That's *my* job.

I'm limiting my criticism to reporters. The responsibility of a reporter is to report the facts so that others can form opinions or make policies. All too often, reporters stray from this responsibility and report the news as they want to view it—with a slant that promotes their own agenda. Admittedly, all reporters have personal views on what they're reporting, but to the extent possible, personal views must be shelved in favor or unbiased reporting.

Bias in mass-media reporting is widespread. I'm talking about mass media reporting, not so-called reporting through social media platforms like *Facebook, Twitter, TikTok,* and the like. Social media platforms are in the embryonic stage of whatever they are to be, and soon will develop sufficient structure deserving of a fitting level of policing.

Underpinning the problems of mass media reporting is that over the past twenty to thirty years, media companies controlling the bulk of media reporting have shrunk from approximately fifty to five or six wealthy and powerful companies, such as Comcast, Disney, National Amusements, News Corp, and one or two others.

One of the flagrant examples of bias in mass media reporting is when events that are reported as facts, too often are reported with a twist and spin, which influences the reader to believe the facts as the reporter wants them viewed. This is not reporting as it should be. This is biased reporting. You don't have to search very hard or far to see examples of biased reporting.

Bias can take many forms. Bias can occur when the reporter places the facts into a location in an article which he or she thinks is more or less important—thus influencing the reader to think in the same manner. For example, facts placed into the last paragraph of an article tend to suggest to readers that such facts have little importance to the substance of the article. Contrarily, a different reporter might cause the placement of those same facts into the headline or first paragraph of an article, intending to influence readers of the importance of *these* facts.

Bias also can be managed by the importance a news media source gives to facts being reported. For instance, certain perceived liberally-oriented newspapers like the *New York Times, Washington Post,* and *USA Today* are less likely to give prime space coverage to articles that might be favorable to Republicans or Conservatives … while *The Wall Street Journal* or the *New York Post* are less likely to give significant prime coverage to articles deemed favorable to Democrats or Liberals.

The size and location of headlines is also considered a method of managing bias. Headlines are perhaps the most read part of any paper, as they immediately capture the reader's attention. So it's no surprise that media sources shape underlying bias by manipulating headlines to highlight facts they want their readers to believe.

So, I'd like to challenge the news media to require that its reporters cease being editorialists … and start reporting facts in an unbiased manner. Leave opinions to the editorialists, who should be duty-bound to label their editorial columns for what they are—opinions and *not* facts.

I will share a few examples of how opinions have infiltrated the field of reporting:

Many news reporters have associated nuclear power with negative reporting, like the reporting on Three Mile Island, Chernobyl, The China Syndrome, nuclear waste, and nuclear weapons. But the scientific community has identified nuclear power as a clean-burning, efficient, and inexpensive alternative to fossil fuels. Who and what should the public believe? Newspapers and media outlets throughout the world should be facilitating and reporting on dialogue setting forth the pros and cons of nuclear power … and letting the public, through the election process and legislatures, decide how nuclear power is developed and to be used.

Another example of biased reporting is in the polarizing attitudes of the news media regarding the Mideast crisis. Reporters should be reporting the facts of what's going on in the Mideast between the Israelis and the Palestinians or in Iran, as well as other players like Hamas and Hezbollah. News articles reporting these events tend to be slanted toward the feelings of those reporting or managing the reporting of the events.

Several mass media publications or entities here in the states are controlled or owned in large part by Jewish persons. Accordingly, the Jewish people have the upper hand in the reporting of events in a manner most favorable to the Israelis. Reporting slanted in favor of Israel not only tends to influence public opinion in the US, but also tends to alienate other Mideast countries with differing views of the facts. Regardless of the issues between Israel and other Mideast countries, isn't it time the media began reporting unbiased facts on the causes for the unrest in the Mideast— instead of attempting to influence public opinion through biased reporting?

Entitlement is another area that reeks of biased reporting. An open discussion by Congress on entitlements is long overdue. Such a dialogue needs to be facilitated by leaders of both major political parties. The media can assist by reporting unbiased facts on the pros and cons of entitlements without interjecting opinion. Let the people have a voice through the election process in deciding the best approach to entitlements.

A more recent example in biased reporting is how certain media sources use their publication to influence public elections. *Time Magazine,* among other news sources, is a good example of having a definite agenda for influencing voters on who should be the next president of the United States. The owners and publishers of newsprint have the right to make their choices known. But biased reporting of a candidate's credentials to influence public opinion should be off limits.

It is undeniable that biases exist. They are caused by natural prejudicial notions that people possess. Everyone sees a set of facts through their own eyes. So, you will never be able to get rid of unintentional bias in the reporting of facts. But intentional bias can be managed and must be eliminated.

The news media needs to work on controlling intentional media bias to bring back credibility to the source. We have a way to go. Until then, it is best for us to be aware that biases exist, and that we should continue to absorb all news with a critical and skeptical eye.

CHAPTER 11

Professor Crum's Final Class

★ ★ ★

Professor Crum was seated in his usual seat at the conference table. His head bobbed up and down several times, and his steely eyes roamed the room piercing the thoughts of his students. The students were aware that this was it … the final session of the course. Typically, students look forward to the last day of a course—but not this course!

Throughout the course, Professor Crum had taken his students on a politically oriented journey, allowing each of them to stop along the way to expose their minds to a reality which would influence them and others as they proceeded through life. He could sense a lingering mist which encircled overhead in the classroom, quietly chanting that the journey the class began had not come to an end. That's what the professor wanted—to take the class down a winding path that eventually would lead to several roads. He was now preparing to leave them, knowing each student now had to make their own decision as to which road to take.

"Let's summarize what we accomplished this semester," said Professor Crum. "We began the course talking generally about politics, our political system, and the presidential candidates for the 2024 presidential election. You told me the important political concerns you thought the presidential candidates should address. You identified fifteen. We discussed them all … thoroughly and maybe too much. We reduced the fifteen concerns into the six most important.

"You thought it was essential that the next president be a person respected and trusted worldwide, and one who would execute the duties and responsibilities of the presidency in a non-partisan way. And you thought the next president should have a reputation for making sound decisions, possess genuine leadership qualities, and possess the desire and capability of uniting our fractured political system so that our government could operate more efficiently. Also, it should be someone who could and would improve the image of the United States both here and abroad. Although there were differing opinions on details, there seemed to be general agreement on the qualifications of the person you would like to see in our next president.

"You examined the leading presidential candidates to see if any might meet your expectations. You thought Joe Biden was too old and feeble to continue to lead our country. You pointed out that Biden has not done an acceptable job in preventing illegal immigrants from entering our country from our southern border. However, you also thought Donald Trump would spend too much time seeking vengeance against those who differ with him in his beliefs, particularly his belief that he won the 2020 presidential election. You all thought Trump has a bullying, impulsive personality, and is a person with a dictatorship type of thought process who seeks personal power and status. You also fear he might not be someone who should be the ultimate decision maker on the use of our nuclear weapons. You accepted as fact that Biden and Trump will be the two candidates who will most likely be the presidential nominees of their respective parties.

"I conducted a straw poll of the class last week asking each of you who you would vote for in the next presidential election. Unless I inaccurately read the results, thirteen of you expressed your choice was 'None of the above.' Two had no opinion. Most of you expressed concern that on Election Day voters will have a choice between two undesirable nominees, both lacking the qualifications you'd like our next president to possess. There appears to be a major disconnect between what the voters deserve and what the voters will receive. So, where do you go from here?"

"What if someone with better qualifications decides to contest Biden and Trump?" said Macey. "Is it too late? What are your thoughts, Professor Crum?"

"My job is over, Macy. My job was to furnish each of you with thinking caps. Some of you still have them on. If you don't like what's happening in front of your eyes, do something about it! All of you have been groomed to be future leaders—so start acting like leaders. Don't ask me what to do. Hell, I don't know!"

"This might sound naive," replied Adam, "but I'm sure there are persons out there who would be better presidential choices than Biden or Trump. Hell, it could even be someone in this class—maybe even you, Crystal. You might make a better president than the one who's likely to be elected."

"Yeah, right," said Liz. "But you have a good point. Chris Christie, Nikki Haley, or Ron DeSantis might be better choices. At least, they say what they think. You might not agree with them, but they present choices. And there are probably others who might be better candidates—for instance, Senator Manchin ... or maybe Bill Gates or Elon Musk. Maybe someone should begin searching for alternatives."

Professor Crum sat back in his chair taking it all in ... seemingly approving what he was hearing. He was witnessing results he had hoped would occur. Most of his students did not want to accept what appeared to be the way the presidential election was heading. He had hoped he was instrumental in his students becoming thinkers, not members of a herd too timid to seek change in the way things are done. The decision among his students to discuss alternatives to the probable presidential nominees was his payoff for teaching the course.

"This is it," said Professor Crum. "As far as I'm concerned, you are all talented individuals ... prepared and ready for what life will bring. There's nothing more you can learn from me or from Duke. But you're not through with me yet. I expect to receive from each of you a *wrap-up paper*. Do you know what a *wrap-up paper* is?"

The class knew what he meant. Professor Crum routinely required from each student a *wrap-up paper* of no more than 500 words, summarizing and assessing what he or she learned in the course (if anything), the relevance of the substance of the course with respect to each student's expectations, an opinion of how the course should be structured in the future to meet the expectations of the next generation of class participants, and an assessment of Professor Crum and the manner in which the course was conducted. The paper was not due until after the class grades were uploaded into Duke's academic records.

No one flunks Professor Crum's course. Why not? First, a person admitted to his class had to be a Political Science major who had fulfilled certain rigid pre-class academic requirements. Then that potential student had to acknowledge and understand that the course was not a lecture course, and that class participation was mandatory. Finally, the course was limited to fifteen students, selected by Professor Crum, all of whom had to submit convincing reasons why they should be picked to attend his class. So a student just didn't flunk his class unless he or she failed to attend classes or refused to participate in class discussions. Most students received an A or B, depending on preparation and willingness to participate.

One by one, the students left the room, each one stopping in front of Professor Crum and in their own way thanking him for his efforts in making the course a meaningful learning experience. And Professor Crum wished them all well. All students had left the room, except Macey, who remained seated in his chair. "I know the course is over, Professor Crum, but I've been thinking about what you said and you're right. Maybe it's not too late to do something."

CHAPTER 12

Islamic Activities

Research Triangle Park, commonly referred to as "The Triangle," is an anchor in North Carolina for the cities of Raleigh, Durham, and Chapel Hill. The universities of Duke, North Carolina State, and North Carolina are located in this region. The Triangle concept was opened as a research park to the public in the late 1950s with a development plan contemplating the presence of many high-tech companies.

For years, Duke University, located in Durham, had been referred to as the Ivy League school of the South. Although it has roots going back to 1838, Duke University, as it is known today, was founded in 1924 by James Buchanan Duke as a tribute to his father, Washington Duke. During the mid-1800s and 1900s, the Washington Duke family built a worldwide financial empire manufacturing tobacco during an environment that advertised the benefits rather than the hazards of smoking. Over the years, the Duke family had been substantial contributors to the university.

Duke University is consistently ranked as one of the top educational and research universities in the United States. Its basketball program also has done well—very well. Its student body presently consists of approximately 6,200 undergraduate students and 10,000 graduate students.

Duke has always been considered predominantly a liberal arts and sciences university. The term "liberal arts" generally describes a college or university curriculum aimed at imparting general knowledge and developing intellectual capacities, in contrast to a professional, vocational, or technical curriculum. A liberal arts education typically offers academic programs that facilitate learning consistent with changing employment opportunities and life experiences in a global society.

Duke's Trinity College has one of the finest liberal arts and sciences programs in the country. Duke also enjoys an excellent reputation for its graduate programs, particularly in the fields of medicine, business, religion, environment, and law.

A liberal-oriented school is not the same as a liberal arts school, but is one that allows its students and faculty broad freedoms of belief within a controlled academic environment. Duke's Trinity College faculty is diverse and now has its share of liberal professors and instructors.

Nowhere could a black undergraduate student attending Duke University in the 1950s be found—not even a black basketball player. Duke's graduate school had a sprinkling of blacks, typically from foreign countries. The school's environment has changed considerably since the early 1960s. Duke's student body now is predominantly multiracial, except in the eyes of those few with minds preconditioned to see racism in virtually every facet of life. Duke now is considered fully and unconditionally racially integrated. Tuition at Duke is pricy, but the same is true with many other institutions with high-priced tuition schedules. However, Duke manages a way to fund tuition for well-qualified, much-in-demand applicants whom the school feels will add to Duke's prestige.

During the past fifty years, the hiring practices for Duke faculty members have been altered dramatically. Over the past twenty years or maybe longer, Duke, a school that had a conservative philosophical leaning faculty, has been transformed to a school with an Arts and

Sciences faculty seemingly ideologically skewed far to the left. To champion and protect the rights of free speech, the Duke administration has bent over backwards to appease critics of our society by offering and making available a forum for its faculty to zealously criticize, in the name of freedom of speech, the values of both Duke and our society.

Duke now has a vibrant African and African American studies program which offers several undergraduate and graduate degrees in areas never considered prior to the mid-1960s. Many wonder whether Duke has not gone too far in offering study programs that tend to encourage the advancement of racial issues, rather than allowing integration among blacks and whites to occur naturally.

Consistent with a pro-active liberal-leaning administration, Duke recently established an Islamic Studies Center, which focuses on undergraduate education and the expansion of Islamic-related educational partnerships with universities in Muslim-populated countries. The Center's ultimate objective is to provide learning with a humanistic approach to the world's future Muslim leaders. The Center seeks to recruit and enroll both undergraduate and graduate student scholars with Muslim backgrounds and beliefs. It also offers fellowships in Islamic studies to graduate students.

With this background, one could easily understand why the organizers of Islamic anti-American activities consider the immediate outskirts of Duke University as a highly desirable location for a regional Islamic terrorist cell group. Foreigners were common folk in and around the Duke campus and in the City of Durham, so effective profiling of radical Islamic followers was virtually impossible. The organizers knew it would be difficult to distinguish between a group of individuals assembled to plan anti-American activities and a group of students with Islamic ties and features assembled for social and educational purposes.

Justin Alabi did not work at Tike's for the money. He had financial support from his native land and his parents had ample money to fund his studies at Duke. Justin had sources in the States that made sure that whatever he wanted to do was not thwarted by reason of lack of funds. For years, Justin had been groomed to play an active role in spreading and enhancing the understanding of Islam in the United States. As a teenager and during school breaks, Justin trained at camps in Pakistan run by the Islamic Jihad Union, a little-known Sunni Muslim group with roots in Uzbekistan and ties to al-Qaida.

It was during those years that he had been pegged by al-Qaida leaders to persist in his studies at a United States university where he could continue his education, while at the same time be positioned as an Islamic emissary. Duke was the school chosen for him. He enrolled in 2020. One of the Duke trustees, Amad Elashi, a Muslim religious leader, was instrumental in having Justin's application for enrollment approved.

The only request made of Justin while attending Duke was for him to think and act like an American, become involved in normal student activities, and develop friends with persons other than Muslims attending Duke, but not to develop a reputation for having radical Islamic views. He was told that he might be asked to meet with a few of his Muslim brothers, if ever requested.

Working part-time at Tike's during his junior and senior years allowed Justin the opportunity to meet all types of Duke students. Occasionally a stranger from outside the Duke area would appear at Tike's during off-peak hours, order a sandwich and a Coke, engage Justin in a quiet conversation, and then leave.

However, the time did come. On Wednesday, October 25, 2023, a person who called himself Malcolm came into Tike's around 6:15 p.m. There were a few customers outside the diner chatting and drinking beer. Malcolm had waited in his car until Justin was alone in the diner.

Then he entered, sat down at a bar stool, ordered a Coke, and asked Justin if he was available on Friday evening to have dinner with Jan Ibala, a visiting professor at Duke.

"Seven o'clock at the Washington-Duke Hotel," requested Malcolm. "Is that OK with you?"

Justin nodded yes and responded, "I'll be there. For whom should I be looking?"

"Professor Ibala knows who you are," said Malcolm. "He'll contact you in the lobby."

Justine Alabi knew that invitation was for real as he had been told his contact while at Duke would bear Justin's last name — spelled backwards.

CHAPTER 13

Washington Duke Inn, Meeting with Professor Ibala

★ ★ ★

The Washington Duke Inn and Golf Course is adjacent to the Duke University campus and is located on Cameron Boulevard in Durham.

It is within walking distance of the campus and Cameron Indoor Stadium, the latter being the site which the new head coach, Jon Schyer, and the Duke basketball team call home.

The Inn sits on well-manicured grounds adjacent to the Duke University Golf Course. A stay at the Inn could be a bit pricy, but the fine dining, upscale environment within and which surround the premises, and the wood and wainscot ambiance throughout the Inn make you feel like you're getting your money's worth. There is no lack of pictures and portraits on the walls to remind one that you are in Duke territory. The Inn and its surroundings complement the Gothic architectural beauty of the buildings on the Duke campus.

Justin parked his 2014 black Lexus SUV in one of the few remaining vacant parking spaces in the area in front of the Inn. It was 6:10 p.m., enough time for him to visit the men's room before meeting with whomever he was to meet. The men's room was to the left of the lobby, between it and the service bar for the two dining areas. At six, Justin strolled through the lobby, waiting to be recognized. The lobby and bar areas were busy with visitors, many appearing to be Duke students and their parents.

"Justin?" said a voice from a large oversized dark-brown-colored leather chair close to where Justin was standing. "Remember me … Malcolm?"

Justin recognized him as the same person who had contacted him at Tikes on Wednesday to arrange the meeting. Malcolm was about six foot one, 205 pounds, with a black moustache and short cropped, bushy black hair. He rose from his chair and extended his hand toward Justin.

"Professor Ibala is expecting you. Please follow me."

Malcolm ushered Justin toward the elevator, which was located to the left and rear of the check-in area. The elevator stopped on the fourth floor. The two continued to Room 427, one of the two luxury suites in the Inn.

Professor *Ibala* was alone in the room when Malcolm knocked. The Professor, casually dressed in a light blue shirt with an open collar and wearing tan sandals, opened the door and greeted Justin as though he had known him for years, which he did in a sense. Though unknown to Justin, Professor Ibala and Amad Khafagi were instrumental in Justin being accepted to Duke as a foreign student.

Justin cautiously entered the room, not knowing what to expect or who would be there. He had been forewarned by Malcolm to speak English and no other language while at the Inn. According to Malcolm, "Americans had a tendency to profile foreigners, particularly those who spoke anything with an Arabic tone."

After exchanging pleasantries, the professor said to Justin: "You know why you're here, don't you?"

"Haven't a clue," said Justin. He was being cautious, although he was fully aware that Professor Ibala was not his real name. He had been told in training camp that his contact while in the States would be someone who called himself a professor with a last name the same as Justin's, except spelled backwards.

"It doesn't matter who I am Justin. Let's just say we've been watching you for several years ... and we think you can help us now. Can we count on you?"

Justin hesitated, realizing his life had changed dramatically over the past few years. His exposure to students with diverse religious backgrounds had softened a few of the radical Islamic beliefs with which he had been indoctrinated. Nevertheless, he responded, "I've been on hold for three years, Professor. How can I help?"

"I'm sure you have heard of Jose Padilla, haven't you?" asked the professor.

"I heard about him while in training," said Justin. "I've read that he had been railroaded into jail. If my memory serves me correctly, wasn't he convicted of setting up a terrorist cell in Miami?"

"That's right. Here in America, they label us *freedom fighters* as terrorists to silence us. He was arrested several years ago and held or as they call it, *detained,* for five years as a wartime criminal, an enemy combatant, and sent to a jail in South Carolina. We retained several lawyers to appeal his conviction. We're seeking a court declaration that Padilla's detention be declared unconstitutional because the US government is not at war with us freedom fighters, so he shouldn't have been held as a wartime prisoner without letting him talk to a lawyer—or at least charging him with a crime.

"Our lawyers tell us it wouldn't hurt our cause to have others support our claim. So far, several university support groups at Harvard,

Yale, Stanford, Cornell, and Columbia have been organized to help us. And that's where you come in. Support from Duke would give us more balanced geographic support on our appeal. Do you think you are up to it?"

Justin wanted to say no—but he didn't. He thought that he was being tested to evidence the degree of his allegiance to the Islamic cause, so he responded, "I'm sure I can help."

The Professor discussed with Justin several ways in which he might be able to help. The professor told Justin that Duke, being more ethnically, politically, and academically diverse than most other universities, has a reputation among the faculty for having many believers in the absolute protection of civil liberties.

"Check out the mood on campus, Justin. See if you can muster up some support. We must act soon."

CHAPTER 14

The Group of Five
Duke Campus
10/28/2023

★ ★ ★

Macey   *Blair*

Group of Five

Liz   *Crystal*

Justin

After Professor Crum's class ended, Macey and many of the other class members hung around outside the classroom building chatting about what Professor Crum was hinting. Macey casually asked if anyone might be interested in further discussions on what Professor Crum said, *"If you don't like the presidential choices, do something about it."*

"The most important job in the world," said Macey, "and look— Trump or Biden. It's sort of like dining out at a five-star restaurant expecting to order an exquisite meal, and then seeing only hash and fried chicken on the menu. Where's the lobster and beef?"

Macey told them he sensed he was not the only one in the class dissatisfied with the presidential contenders. "Lots of promises ... very few solutions," he said. "The candidates are programmed to say whatever it takes to get elected. Trump is so cocky that he'll be the Republican nominee, he refused to participate in any of the Republican debates scheduled for TV."

Several thought Macey was overreacting to the reality of politics, and, though not differing with his thoughts, didn't want to get involved in something they thought would go nowhere. Two of the class members said flatly that they just didn't care who became president.

Only Blair Durtz, Crystal Brown, Zada Nogah, Liz Reicher, and Justin Alabi evidenced any interest in what Macey was saying. Therefore, the six agreed to meet the next morning at the Bryan Center to explore further interest.

The next morning, Zada didn't show up for the meeting. She had decided not to get involved. The remaining five acknowledged there were many hurdles to leap, but decided to consider searching for alternate candidates they believed had the qualifications and beliefs the next president of the United States should possess.

The first decision they made was to refer to themselves as the Group of Five. The Group then discussed what their objectives would be. "We should set reasonable goals as to what we hope to accomplish," said Liz.

All five agreed the next president should be a decision-maker, and a person who would be respected and trusted by political leaders here and abroad. Additionally, the Group agreed the next president should possess genuine leadership qualities and have the capability of uniting a fractured partisan political system. This candidate should also have the courage to meet with Congressional members of all parties to remind them of their duty as elected officials to make non-partisan legislative decisions which are best for the country.

The Group recognized the list of potential alternative choices would be limited, and probably would not be anyone within the political ranks. After two hours of discussion, only the name Hugo McCormick had surfaced as a serious contender. No member of the Group knew Hugo personally, but thought they knew enough about his character and credentials from reading many of his editorials.

According to the Group of Five, Hugo seemed to possess many, if not most, of the qualifications they were looking for as an alternative to Biden and Trump. So they decided Hugo would be targeted as a possible alternative to a new president.

CHAPTER 15

Indian River Book Store, Book Presentation
10/29/2023

★ ★ ★

Kara

Kara Fitzgibbons, owner of Indian River Bookstore in Vero Beach, Florida, was already at the wood veneer orator podium sipping coffee from a blue, orange, and green-colored mug with the word "GATORS" inscribed on the side. She was in good spirits. The speaker's room, located in the back of her store, was packed. Kara had attracted a well-known personality to present a book recently published entitled, *No More Small Talk.*

It was five minutes to ten. The author, Hugo McCormick, was seated to the right of the podium behind a small, rectangular, solid oak table, which had nothing on top of it except an unopened plastic bottle of Zephyrhills Spring Water, a yellow legal pad, two non-descript black ballpoint pens, a small tape recorder, and a large pile of unsigned books.

Hugo, a person generally very much in control of his emotions, appeared a bit fidgety. This was new to him. He had never been on a book tour before, and probably never would again. However, his publisher strongly recommended he at least make one or two appearances to jumpstart the sale of his book.

Hugo wrote the book to express the political thoughts he expressed while in Congress, but nobody listened. Hugo picked the Indian River Book Store to jump-start the sale only because the temperature in Vero Beach was much warmer than in Connecticut and he had an opportunity to play golf with old friends in the area. However, most important to him was that he had received a telephone call from Kara six weeks ago. He had promised her he would do a presentation and book signing at her store shortly after the book was published. Twenty-one years earlier, Kara had been active in Hugo's run for Congress. Though she was an insignificant factor in his being elected, she did help. Now she saw the opportunity to lean on this shallow relationship to bring a few new customers to her store.

Most of the 115 people who had crowded into the back room of Kara's store were seated in rows of soft-cushioned folding chairs. The chairs were positioned to form a broad semicircle around the podium. A few attendees were still jostling and positioning for seats when Kara started speaking.

"It's now ten and I promised our distinguished guest I would start on time. He made it clear he had a two o'clock tee time at Grand Harbor, and I didn't want him to miss the opportunity to have his trip partially subsidized by a couple of his old cronies now living in the area.

"First, I want to thank you all for attending what should be an enlightening hour and a half with our guest speaker. I know many of you have been present at one or more of our prior book presentations, but for those who haven't, let me outline the agenda. I will introduce our guest. He will speak about his book for approximately forty-five minutes.

"Then there will be a question-and-answer period of, say, thirty minutes. After that, if anybody is interested in purchasing his book, and I hope you all will, our guest might be talked into hanging around a bit longer to sign copies. Any questions?"

Kara glanced around the room not expecting any questions. Seeing none, she looked over at her guest to make sure he was ready to proceed. Hugo gave her a thumbs-up.

Kara then began her introduction of Hugo. "As you all know or you probably wouldn't be here, my guest is the Honorable Hugo McCormick. I call him Honorable not because he once served as a congressman from the state of Connecticut, but more importantly because he is an honorable man. He tells me he hates to be addressed as Honorable—he would rather be called Hugo. So our guest is Hugo—Hugo McCormick. Let me tell you a little about him.

"I worked for Hugo's campaign in 2002 when he was running for Congress. I won't say I had any impact on his being elected, but I did get a few relatives to vote for him. He probably didn't know who I was at the time, but I knew everything about him.

"Hugo went through the public schools in West Haven, Connecticut, graduated from Duke University in 1975, and then attended The University of Connecticut School of Law, graduating in 1978. He practiced law in the New Haven-West Haven area for about twenty-three years prior to running for Congress.

Hugo left Congress after two terms, choosing not to seek a third. After Congress, for reasons known only by Hugo, he decided not to return to the practice of law. Rather, he began an entirely new career in journalism as an editorialist with *The Hartford Globe*. For those not familiar with The *Globe*, it is a Hartford, Connecticut-based daily newspaper with a broad readership in the New England states. Hugo's editorial columns opened a few eyes and his weekly editorials are now syndicated to newspapers throughout the United States.

"If you have read any of Hugo's editorials, then I don't have to tell you he speaks from the heart, doesn't mince words, and he doesn't tap dance around difficult issues. Unlike many political figures, he speaks the language of the common man in clear, simple and unambiguous language—language which even I can understand.

He has a set of core values and beliefs which have resulted in him becoming one of the most popular, admired, and respected men. Those familiar with Hugo and his editorials most certainly will agree that he has earned a reputation for speaking for the people. After this buildup, you might say to yourself, why is he a politician? Well, he isn't. Not anymore. He's a journalist—and now a journalist and an author. Without further ado, I am pleased to introduce Hugo McCormick."

The audience politely applauded while Hugo rose and took several steps to the podium. Most of the attendees were familiar with Hugo's columns and came to see him and listen to what he had written in his book.

"Thanks for the flattering remarks, Kara," said Hugo. "And thank you all for attending. No ... I did not write Kara's introductory script. In fact, I didn't even know who she was talking about until she mentioned my name. And yes, Kara, though you were much younger than me when I ran for Congress, I do remember you from my campaign. If my memory serves me accurately, you're the one who always wore those worn-out jeans with the designer holes in the knees."

Kara cringed, and her face turned bright red. The audience burst out with laughter, which Kara feared might later be echoed in kind by many of her friends in attendance.

"First, I will tell you why I wrote the book and then I'll briefly discuss the content.

"I was elected to Congress in 2002. Prior to that, I had practiced law in my hometown of West Haven, Connecticut for about twenty-three years. At that time, I had no real political aspirations. I was a registered Democrat back then, not because of political ideologies, but because the Democrats were in control of the city and my law partner represented the city as corporate counsel.

"I was asked to run for Congress by the Independent Party. At the time, many voters in the 7th Congressional District were dissatisfied with their lack of creative choices. I agreed with this assessment and let my thoughts be known. To my surprise, after much effort and hard work by my campaign staff—people like Kara—I was elected. My initial thoughts were, 'Wow! What an opportunity.' I had big dreams about how I would change things when I arrived in Washington. I was pumped up. Inertia in Washington would be a thing of the past during my watch. How wrong I was!

"You don't really understand politics until you've been handed the job of being a politician. I wanted so much to live up to my campaign promises. How naive I was to think others would pay attention to anything I had to say. As a rookie in Congress, since I wasn't a member of one of the major political parties, my voice could hardly be heard. I was assigned an office—a very small office—conveniently out of the way, so you needed a map to find me. To my chagrin, I was treated like a first-year pledge who had to wait his turn to be accepted into the political fraternal society. I felt like an outcast—I was an outcast.

"I spent most of my time with minutia, and rarely was consulted, unless one of the party leaders needed my vote on a matter where my vote meant something. It didn't take long for me to realize that Washington politics is a game where you must belong to a major political party to play, and then you either play by partisan rules or you don't play at all.

"I'm sorry to say that too many of my fellow brethren played by partisan rules, prioritizing whatever his or her party said had to be done, rather than pursuing issues that might make things better for you and me. I couldn't operate within these tacit rules, so after two terms, I opted out.

"My brief stay in Washington taught me a few things:

1. Politicians either do not recognize or choose not to recognize many important issues for political or personal reasons.

2. Politicians spend far too much time on partisan investigative committees and hearings, most of which target activities of members of the opposing party.

3. Congressmen tend to vote by party line rather than on the merits of proposed legislation, a practice that has paralyzed Congressional action. Democrats find it difficult to support legislation sponsored by Republicans, and Republicans find it equally as difficult to support legislation sponsored by Democrats. And there are extremists in both parties, each having their own agenda.

"Bottom line, in my view, is that the culture of legislators serving in Congress needs to be changed. There is a real need for Congressional legislators to reject party-line politics and work together on important matters needing Congressional action. Our next president needs to tear down the barrier between the major political parties and exert leadership to make this happen.

"I left office with the feeling that I had let down the voters who had supported me. I went to Washington with high hopes, and left wondering how I could have been a more effective representative. I didn't have answers. That's what led me into doing what I do now—

pursue a career where my voice is not any louder, but now might be heard. That's why I wrote my book, *No More Small Talk*."

Hugo paused to take a sip of water—and while doing so, a few persons in the audience began applauding. The applause became contagious until almost everyone in the audience was rhythmically clapping and standing to express appreciation for Hugo's candor, admission of ineptness, and his commitment to prod members of Congress from a different direction.

"Thank you, thank you. I don't know for what, but thanks.

"What is *No More Small Talk* about? Well, I've been writing and speaking for years on those social, political, and economic issues too often ignored by our elected officials. We elect officials to represent us, to tackle the problems of the day, and to pursue legislation beneficial to you, me, and our society. But our interests often take a back seat to matters seemingly more important to the people we elected.

"Our political system is so partisan-based now that Congress had routinely struggled to muster up the required number of votes to pass the Government's annual budget—a budget that requires congressional approval to avoid a government shutdown!

"And recently, the Republicans, who have controlling votes in the House, couldn't even get enough votes from their own party to elect a House Speaker. This resulted in the Government being without a House Speaker for several weeks during a period when it should have been addressing critical issues.

"Clearly, those whom we elect to office need to better represent the people who elect them, and not disregard us voters by acting in a partisan manner. Voting the party line has become a priority over what's right for us voters. So I write to give a voice to the many persons who want to see responsible action on legislative matters from our elected officials. I write to encourage and prod non-partisan dialogue by the members of all parties, Democrats, Republicans, and Independents, on matters which directly or indirectly impact our daily lives."

Hugo then pointed to an elderly female in the first row and said, "Ma'am, let me pick on you. I don't know you, but I'd say you're probably retired and a Florida resident."

She nodded, yes. "And I'd say that property taxes and insurance are very important to you—maybe health care?" She again nodded, yes.

"And you," he said, pointing to a middle-aged young man in a second-row aisle seat, "I'd say you also might be concerned with property taxes and insurance, but you might have equal or greater concerns about crime, drugs, and civil rights—maybe even global warming?

"Whatever, all of us have concerns that are important to us—concerns that may change in importance as we get older and our lives change. It is these concerns that you expect will be addressed by the people you voted into office.

"If the candidate for whom you voted gets elected and then either ignores or doesn't make a genuine effort to do what they promised, you get angry and frustrated—and that's probably it. Most of you are unable to do anything but complain. Well, not me! I'm too stubborn.

"I certainly don't want to give the impression that all politicians are cut from the same cloth. No, many are good legislators, caring and well-intentioned. But important legislative matters often don't move because party leaders demand partisan voting by a party member—or face being ostracized.

"As an editorialist, and now an author of sorts, I'm able to bring pressure on legislators to recognize and have a dialogue about matters which I believe requires transparency and decision-making. You folks can help by communicating with the elected officials for whom you voted whenever you're dissatisfied on matters important to you. If you're dissatisfied, you can either continue to pressure your elected officials to take certain actions or vote them out of office in hopes of electing more favorable replacements.

"My book includes my thoughts and opinions on the many social, economic, and political matters that, in my view, are important to all of us and need to be addressed by Congress and our president.

"You might ask what I consider important matters for Presidential or Congressional action—fair question. Well, with what's happening now in the Mideast, in Ukraine, and our tenuous relationships with China, Russia, Iran, and North Korea, I think national security and world peace are high on the list. What are we doing to best protect the interests of our country? What role should the United States play in seeking a path to world peace?

"With so many other economic and financial problems competing for government funding, how much longer can we afford to have a military presence in so many countries? Is our presence on foreign soil appreciated ... or desired? Are we heading in a direction leading to a nuclear war, an event that might affect civilization as we know it?"

Hugo continued, "Terrorism—we can't hide from it. What is the cause of worldwide terrorism? How do we deal with the increasing threat of terrorism? What role should we play in controlling or eliminating terrorism? Can we peacefully co-exist with religious radical Islamic groups that flatly state they seek the elimination or religious submission of Christians and Jews? These are important concerns that must be recognized and addressed."

Hugo took another sip of water, but he was not through. He was on a roll.

"What about poverty here in the United States and abroad? How long will it be before the increasing income gap between *the haves* and *the have-nots* in our country reaches a point where the have-nots decide it's time to unite and forcefully demand a bigger share of the American Dream?

"Is the rise in gangs and crime in America in any way attributable to the increasing income gap between the haves and have-nots? If so, shouldn't we be focusing on narrowing this gap while we can do so in a controlled manner? I certainly can understand why politicians do not want to touch this issue. It's a tough one. But tough decisions by legislators come with the turf.

"We need a sensible basic health care program, one that is affordable and available for all Americans. Health care should not be seen in terms of *them against us*. Americans no longer are *looking* for a health care solution—they are *demanding* one. How do we accomplish this in a responsible and entrepreneurial manner so our government doesn't go broke? How involved should the Federal Government be in implementing a basic health care program?

"We need a bipartisan solution that incorporates health care entitlement philosophies of both the Republican and Democratic parties. We need more than dialogue here—we need action. We have no choice other than to demand a non-partisan solution to what is a basic need; that is, unless we are prepared for an uncontrolled, mass societal shakeup.

"How big should the Federal Government be? How much power should it have? Both Democrats and Republicans and the layers within their respective parties have made the issue of the size of the Federal Government a cornerstone ideological difference. That's fine. There are areas where our federal government arguably might be a better manager of certain entitlement programs—areas where the private sector would prefer to yield authority to *Big Brother,* such as *basic* health care and retirement benefits to all citizens.

"However, we must be careful not to allow the Federal Government to step on the toes of the private sector. We want the private sector to continue to be involved with health care and retirement benefits beyond the basic core benefits. We don't want *Big Brother* to discourage entrepreneurial instincts when it comes to rewarding employees with over and above basic benefits. Entrepreneurs lie at the heart of innovation and the reward system. So, we need dialogue to develop a bi-partisan plan for the role the Federal Government should play in specific phases of our lives.

"Something must be done about the disparity in income levels. We have seen a wart grow in our society which has resulted in a financial reward system that has lost touch with the working class. Rock stars, athletes, and greedy CEOs are reaping financial rewards far greater than the reasonable value of the services performed, particularly when compared to the incomes received by our policemen, firemen, teachers, and many blue-collar workers.

"We need to find a way to continue to encourage both motivation and private sector entrepreneurship to succeed, while still putting limits on those outlandish financial rewards that make a mockery of the salaries of so many who can't afford to live beyond the poverty level.

"What do we do? I don't know. But I do know that if we don't address this issue soon, a remedy might just be forced down our throats by forces we have yet to experience here in America. So we need dialogue on income disparity. We need to find a way to put more money in the pockets of low-income persons and families.

"And how should civil liberties be balanced? We don't want to profile. We don't want to infringe on our constitutionally driven civil liberties. But there IS a limit. Where the safety and security of our country is at stake, certain liberties need to be curtailed. Should illegal immigrants be entitled to the same civil liberty protections as those applicable to citizens of the United States? Issues flowing from the massive influx of immigrants at our borders mandate a review of how civil liberties are to be interpreted and enforced.

"I think we need responsible dialogue in all the areas I mentioned previously. Don't we elect members of Congress for the purpose of legislating on such important matters? If so, why do so many legislators devote much of their time in Washington performing seemingly meaningless things, like serving on committees investigating members of the other party over seemingly partisan trivia?

"By the looks on your faces, I can sense that most of you are thinking, 'Does this guy have a political agenda? Are his views more political than practical? Is he a nut case?' I hope I have convinced more than a few that I *do* make sense. I don't want to appear to be an alarmist—I'm merely pointing out important issues that beg to be addressed by both Congress and our President—but aren't. You can't allow those you voted into office to ignore their job.

"I have no political agenda or income-generating motive. I'm not running for office, nor do I intend to do so. And I'll be giving my portion of the proceeds from the sale of my book to charitable organizations.

"I want to thank all of you for listening to me for the past forty-five minutes. If you have any questions or comments, I will be glad to respond—after I take a brief break."

CHAPTER 16

Indian River Book Store, After the Break

★ ★ ★

After a ten-minute break, Hugo returned to the podium, took a sip of water, and prepared to respond to six or seven hands that had popped up from different areas of the room. Hugo expected there would be questions. Why shouldn't there be? He had saturated the minds of those in attendance with thoughts that begged for an explanation, clarification, or discussion.

Hugo pointed his index finger to acknowledge a middle-aged female, dressed in designer jeans, a Lily-print, lime green and pale-yellow colored shirt, which matched her tightly cropped yellowish-white hair. "Mr. McCormick, my name is Joan Walz. I live here in Vero Beach. I think we all want to live in a peaceful world ... but aren't you asking us to believe in a utopian world?"

Hugo's eyes roamed throughout the room, while nodding his head to signify his anticipation that someone would ask that question. "Good question. And I'll be more than happy to give you my thoughts.

"World peace: can world peace ever be attained? Perhaps not in an absolute sense, but shouldn't we strive for the ultimate, and then be prepared to accept something a bit less? What world peace means can only be measured by the expectations in the eyes of those seeking the answer. In my opinion, it means living in an international environment where people and countries honor and respect each other's form of government, their territorial limits, their respective customs and religious beliefs, their social and economic philosophies, and their way of life. Our planet is much smaller than it was one to two hundred years ago. Not in terms of size, but in terms of travel, communication, ideologies, technologies, cultures, and economies. Slowly, life on our planet is becoming an integrated society in terms of race and cultures. In a sense, the world rapidly is becoming a melting pot for all cultures and beliefs.

"Global peace will never be seen by you or me, so long as our world leaders refuse to recognize the forest from the trees. What do I mean by that? The forest is the Earth, and the trees are the total population of all countries occupying our planet. Our world leaders should resist fighting each other over relatively less important concerns, like territorial borders, religious views, and differing governing philosophies. Rather, world leaders should recognize the need to work together against forces which could materialize into catastrophic events causing serious changes to both the forest *and* the trees—maybe even causing the end of civilization here on our planet.

"How important is territorial grabbing or religious wars if a large meteorite or other enormous mass were to slam into Earth, destroying most if not all its inhabitants? Or if the sun suddenly began losing the fuel from surrounding gases it feeds on, to the extent it no longer can sufficiently warm or light our Earth? Or how about if our planet was invaded by persons or creatures from a different planet or if a nuclear war begins among the major countries? What if life on Earth was threatened by the extinction of mankind from a worldwide contagious, uncontrollable deadly disease? I'm sure there are more events lingering out there that, if not addressed by world leaders as a group, they could someday affect life here on Earth—but I think you get my point.

"If ever we are to experience global peace, world leaders must look beyond the cultural characteristics that define differences between one country from another and focus as a group on what needs to be done to protect civilization from extraordinary, catastrophic events. If world leaders were to do so, just maybe wars between countries would become meaningless, and countries now harboring differing races, cultures, religious, economic and social beliefs, and governing philosophies might just look beyond the trees to save a forest seeking to be protected."

A voice from the rear of the room yelled out in a somewhat argumentative tone, "I generally agree with you, Hugo. World peace is important. But I think it's important for the president and other world leaders to understand the reasons why certain countries will never be able to get along with others, and then address those reasons."

Hugo responded, "I don't disagree. Understanding and accepting the need for an environment whereby people of different races, religious beliefs, and customs can live side by side is an essential start to a path leading to world peace. Global peace as an issue is near the top of the pile for the next president to address."

The same voice from the back of the room asked whether Hugo thought conflicting views by religious groups might be a roadblock to world peace.

Hugo responded, "We are making inroads in the general acceptance of diversity of religious beliefs. Clearly, there are many similarities in the core beliefs and practices of Christianity, Judaism, and Islam. Sure, there are extremists who frown on religious diversity. But I am pleased to see that universities in the United States and abroad now are encouraging and promoting interfaith dialogue groups by fostering awareness of religious pluralism and diversity.

"Christians, Jews, Muslims, and Hindus are encouraged to meet, not for purposes of promoting conversion of others to a particular religion, but to exchange thoughts and acquire an appreciation for and acceptance of the religious beliefs of others. Universities who offer and promote such programs have made great strides toward healing religious and political differences. This is a giant step toward achieving world peace."

Hugo then acknowledged in the back row the tentatively raised hand of a young mother who was attending the book presentation with a two year-old hanging onto her arm. "Hi, Hugo, my name's Sophia. I live in Palm Bay—not far from here, and I have two pre-school children. World peace is important, but right now I'm more concerned about crime and the

Sophia

youth gangs in our neighborhood. I worry about the safety of my kids. How are these problems being addressed?"

"I think you should be concerned, Sophia—as should our government. Crime, drugs, and the increase of inner-city youth gangs are major social issues. We need to understand why our youth needs to resort to crime and gangs, rather than seeking an education or getting a job. We no longer can afford to just talk about these problems—we need to understand causes, and then tackle those causes. I don't have the solutions, Sophia, but the solutions are there. We need to find them."

"What about drugs?" questioned Sophia. "When growing up in Connecticut, many of my classmates had easy access to pot and other forms of drugs. It's worse now, and I fear what my kids will be exposed to. Why are you in favor of legalizing drugs?"

"Perhaps you read one of my editorials on drugs?" inquired Hugo. "We must accept the fact that illegal drugs are a big business, especially for our federal government. However, it's a much bigger business for organized crime. Street drugs are expensive, because they are illegal and drug lords and gangs kill and maim to control drug trafficking.

"In many foreign countries and maybe even in our own, prosecutors are disinclined to prosecute drug charges, judges are reluctant to punish them, and witnesses are hesitant to testify about drug trafficking activities. The more important question is why? Too many innocent persons have been assassinated, tortured, or maimed for prosecuting or testifying against drug trafficking activities.

"In several South American countries, drug lords have more sophisticated weaponry than the governments in those countries who are in charge of policing illegal drugs. What drives the illegal drug trade is demand and the high price dealers can charge for them. The money paid to dealers on all levels apparently is enough to offset the risk of being caught. Far too many persons, including young members of gangs, view drug dealing as a more profitable pursuit than either not working or working forty hours a week at minimum wage."

"Can't we stiffen the penalties for the dealers?" asked Sophia.

"We could and have done so many times," answered Hugo, "but that hasn't worked so far. Our jail system already is bursting at the seams with drug dealers. I think we need a solution that goes to the core of the problem. My solution is to legalize the purchase and sale of all drugs, except for certain powerful drugs to teenagers."

Half of the audience looked surprised at what Hugo was saying. The other half appeared intrigued. Hugo paused for a moment, knowing he was touching on a sensitive topic which many persons might have sharply different views. But that's the way he saw things, so he decided to continue.

"What will legalizing the sale and purchase of drugs do?" asked Hugo. "For starters, there no longer will be a need for an illegal distribution channel. As a result, gangs that had been formed to deal in drugs will be stripped of their own importance and purpose. If drugs are manufactured and distributed legally, illegal drug prices would drop significantly, lessening the motivation to become or remain drug dealers. There would also be a precipitous end to wars among the drug lords, dealers, and drug enforcement agencies.

"And, if the sale of drugs is no longer illegal, we could reduce substantially the number of persons presently in the federal and state drug enforcement agencies. Prosecutor's offices could trim their respective staffs as the criminal drug caseloads would be reduced substantially. Jails would become less crowded."

A dark-haired young lady in the first row, visibly upset and vigorously shaking her head in a direction suggesting disbelief about what Hugo had just said, stood up and called out above the murmuring of the audience, "But if we legalize the use of drugs, aren't we inviting use by those who otherwise wouldn't experiment with drugs, particularly teenagers? I have five teenaged kids. If drugs are legal to purchase, wouldn't we be sending a message that might encourage abuse?"

"Fair question," answered Hugo. "Legalizing drugs is not the panacea for illegal drugs. But think about it. We plan to spend over twenty billion dollars this year to promote a policy of enforcement and punishment. Why not spend this money to support drug treatment and a meaningful education program. Why continue to subsidize an operation where organized crime is the primary beneficiary?"

"I read an article recently," commented Sophia, "that suggested organized crime has threatened several of our legislators if they pursue the legalization of drugs. Is this true?"

"Well, I wasn't one of the legislators, Sophia. I'm not aware of others. But I wouldn't be surprised. My solution is simple. Eliminate the incentives for dealing in illegal drugs, and then concentrate on educating those who need to be educated on the pitfalls of using harmful drugs. As far as our youth are concerned, we should continue with laws prohibiting the sale of drugs to minors."

"What about the use of enhancement drugs by professional athletes?" asked a middle-aged, stocky male, with dark sunglasses topping a cap advertising *New River Marina,* and wearing a pink monogrammed sweatshirt that looked like it needed washing. "How do you justify this use?"

"You sound like a doctor," answered Hugo. "Let's look at what Roger Clemens went through. Did he use body enhancement drugs? Maybe yes. Maybe no. The Hall of Fame Committee apparently thinks he did. What about those who use Viagra or Cialis—for when the moment is right? How many of us are hooked on and need caffeine to get ready for the upcoming events of the day? How many reach for a Dewar's or Chardonnay or Bass Ale in the evening to relax after a busy day? Or those addicted to nicotine, who depend on its use to relax during stressful moments? How about those energy-boosting drinks to enhance performance on the tennis courts or while running the half-marathon?

"Isn't our use of all these mind-altering substances a matter of personal choice? Is there a difference between fans at a sporting event being stoned on alcohol, while watching a performing athlete juiced with steroids? Isn't the sensation the same for the one *scoring* with the use of Viagra as it is for the one who scores a touchdown with the use of steroids? Shouldn't the user of an enhancement drug be the judge as to whether the benefits of the drug, legal or illegal, outweighs the negative effect the drug might have on his or her own body—provided no one else is harmed and the consequences from the use of the drug are self-sustained?"

Out of the corner of his eye, Hugo saw Kara pointing to her watch, signaling him that he should consider bringing his presentation to a close.

"I see that I've already taken too much of your time, so I'll bring my presentation to an end. Thanks for coming and listening to a few issues that I believe need more thought and transparency. I hope I have given you cause and incentive to think about things that are happening in our world."

Before Hugo could ease away from the podium, a young but loud voice could be heard resounding from the rear of the room, "Mr. McCormick, one last question. Why don't you run for President? We could use some fresh ideas. I'm having a hard time deciding who to vote for as our next president. Right now, it's none of the above."

"Thanks, but NO thanks," said Hugo. "I had my chance in Washington, but I was useless there. I'm more effective on the sidelines. I will continue exercising my self-designated responsibility of urging our elected officials to have dialogues and offer solutions to the real problems of the world.

"You too have a responsibility if you feel short-changed by the people you elected to office. You have the responsibility to vote for the person who will best represent your beliefs. You can't allow politicians to get away with ignoring your concerns."

While Kara walked to the podium, the audience stood and gave Hugo much more than polite applause—seemingly pleased by his willingness to say what was on his mind, and by ending his presentation with motivational and inspirational remarks.

CHAPTER 17

Barbecue at Professor Crum's House
11/4/2023

★ ★ ★

Maddie Crum exclusively purchases her barbecue from Lexington Barbecue, a small diner on Route 64 in Lexington, North Carolina. The diner makes its own barbecue, western North Carolina style, also known as Lexington Style. The diner is a small, out-of-the-way place, but had the *best barbecue around*, or so thought Maddie. The diner was famous for its barbecue in North Carolina and its bordering states—some say in the United States. When Maddie purchased barbecue, she purchased enough for several hefty meals.

Lexington Barbecue, as most in the area knew, is made from pork shoulders and a *Special Sauce* made with a heavy ketchup and vinegar base, a small dose of sugar, and pretty much anything else the maker considered suitable to constitute his special sauce. Pork shoulders are less fatty than other meat from the hog, and reputedly have more texture than the whole-hog pork meat used in eastern North Carolina.

Most Duke freshmen from states other than the Carolinas, Tennessee, and Virginia never had the opportunity to taste serious barbecue. Macey was introduced to this southern dish early on, and barbecue became one of his favorite meals—along with steak, lobster, fish, chicken, and whatever else could be found on a restaurant menu.

On Thursday night, Macey called Professor Crum and asked if he had time to meet to discuss a few things. "Just want to pick your brain, Professor," said Macey.

Professor Crum was not overly surprised to hear Macey's voice. His course was over, the grades already had been turned in, so he knew Macey wanted to discuss something other than the "A" he soon would learn he would receive for the course. "I'm free Saturday evening," responded the professor. "How about dinner at my house, say 6:30?" Macey accepted the invitation.

The Crums lived on a nonworking farm in an 1876, white, historical house in Durham, close to the Duke campus. The three, Maddie, Professor Crum, and Macey, sat around a small, round, antique oak table located in a dining area adjoining the Crum's large country-style kitchen. Lexington barbecue was the main meal.

Maddie served the barbecue, surrounded by a container of Lexington Barbecue's Special Sauce, a vinegar-based coleslaw, chips, and dill pickles served on a large platter. In the center of the table, Maddie placed a basket of fresh warm rolls, and next to that she served her special three-cheese macaroni dish, a dish not known for lacking calories.

Macey never met Maddie before, so the two carried the dinner conversation, most of which centered on Macey, his family, his background, and why he chose Duke to pursue an education. Professor Crum sat and listened, content to see his wife taking an interest in the life of one of his students.

After dinner, Maddie excused herself, leaving her husband and Macey to talk. "I'll be upstairs," said Maddie. "Let me know if you need anything. Nice meeting you, Macey."

Professor Crum and Macey remained seated. The professor had just poured himself a cup of decaf. "Never drink the strong stuff before bed," he said. Macey declined the decaf saying, "Never touch the weak stuff, ever." He was satisfied with drinking the remainder of the beer he had with his dinner.

The two proceeded to chat for almost two hours. Macey began the conversation explaining why he wanted to talk. "Several of us from your class have been meeting for the past week. You put a bug in our ears. You made us think—maybe we shouldn't be content with Biden and Trump being the only nominees for president. Maybe we should stop complaining and do something about it."

"Hmmm, interesting, Macey," commented the professor. "Lots of folks out there are complaining about the same thing, but don't know what to do. So, what are your thoughts?"

"Remember in class how we discussed the qualifications we'd like to see in our next president, and then listed issues and concerns we thought our next president should address. Look at our probable choices. Biden is 81 and it's clear his health and mental status will affect his ability to handle the pressures of the presidency for four more years. According to Trump, Biden's immigration policies have resulted in the United States being referred to as the 'dumping ground of the world.' I don't disagree.

"What's the alternative to Biden? Donald Trump! He's the frontrunner, considered by the press to be the leader of the Republican Party, and most likely will be the Republican nominee. But his popularity beyond those of the MAGA cult has soured over the past few years. He is considered by many, including me, to be impulsive, explosive, a threat to our Constitution, and a person many would prefer not to be making decisions on the use of nuclear weapons. It's unpredictable what would happen if Trump was in charge of government administrators and agencies of whom he has severely criticized since he left office. Our group is particularly concerned that Trump will say almost anything to become re-elected. If he does become elected, he may spend too much time seeking revenge against those critical of him during and after his first term in office.

"So our group—we now call ourselves the Group of Five—decided we should look for an alternative candidate to challenge the probable Democratic and Republican nominees."

"Isn't this where we left off?' asked the professor.

"Right!" said Macey. "However, now we have someone in mind and we'd appreciate your help."

Professor Crum leaned back in his chair with his hands clasped together behind his neck and focused his eyes on the ceiling. Then he stared at Macey, looking him square in the eyes, "What do you want me to say, Macey? That I approve of what you're thinking? Sure I do. But I can't assist you in the process."

"We're not asking you to get involved in the selection process, Professor. We figured you wouldn't. All we ask is that you serve as a sounding board as we proceed. We may not get to first base in our efforts, but we all agreed to proceed to the next level."

"Who do you have in mind?" inquired the professor.

"You might know him. His name is Hugo McCormick. He's a journalist. Ever hear of him?"

"Hugo McCormick? Sure," he answered. "I don't know him personally, but I like him. I read his columns religiously. If you're looking for a person who is candid and opinionated, you don't have to look much further. If I can recall, he served in Congress years ago. Have you talked with him?"

"No," replied Macey. "I met him a few years ago when I was in prep school. My father hired him after he left Congress … about seventeen years ago. My dad owns the newspaper where he works."

"I didn't know that, Macey. So, you do have a connection. Will he run?"

"Haven't the faintest idea. Our group considered him the best choice. Is he perfect? — Probably not, but he does measure up to most of what we've been looking for in a president. And he's the only person upon which we all agreed. We'd like to talk with him, and thought you could help."

"I said I like his line of thinking," commented the Professor, "but you know I can't take sides on political issues. How effective would I be as a political science professor if I allowed my personal views to taint classroom thinking? Sorry, Macey. I just can't get involved."

"Again, I'm not asking you to take a political position, Professor. Even though he works for my father, Mr. McCormick probably wouldn't pay attention to me. In his eyes, I'm still a young punk."

Professor Crum smacked his lips, shook his head from side to side, and rolled his eyes, suggesting he knew he shouldn't get involved, but thinking—what the heck!

Macey saw that he was making progress with Professor Crum, so thought a bit of flattery might help. "You carry a bit more weight than we do, Professor. He might at least talk to you. You don't have to do anything other than ask him to meet with a few of your students to discuss politics and political strategies. No heavy agenda. Just open the door and leave the rest to us. Will you help?"

Professor Crum thought for a moment, and then said, "I won't say no right now. I'll give it some thought."

The Hartford Globe

CHAPTER 18

The Hartford Globe - Hartford, Connecticut
11/6/2023

★ ★ ★

Hugo had been away from his office for three days. His desk, though usually uncluttered, was now piled up with unopened correspondence and a stack of telephone messages from persons who apparently did not want to leave a voice message.

The messages and letters were put on his desk by Elaine, his part-time secretary, who had worked for Hugo for six years. She always knew where he was and what he should be doing. Hugo emphatically informed her on several occasions that he was not to be contacted outside the office on matters which did not appear urgent. None of the letters or phone messages appeared to be urgent.

The letters were from fans and non-fans. Most of the correspondence was complimentary or had positive things to say about whatever Hugo had written. A few messages challenged his thoughts, while a few others were outright mean. But Hugo had grown thick skin since leaving Congress, and negative correspondence no longer bothered him—at least, that's what he wanted people to believe.

Hugo checked his voice messages daily, even when out of the office. He responded immediately to friends or acquaintances or to those leaving urgent messages worthy of response. Hugo had five Voicemail messages from persons he didn't know. One raised his curiosity. The call was from Professor Eric Crum of Duke University. The message was left on November 5th and said, "Congressman McCormick. This is Eric Crum. You don't know me, but I'm a professor at Duke. A group of my students asked me to contact you. They would like to meet you to discuss a class project they're working on. Please give me a call. I can be reached at (919) 680-2705."

Hugo had heard of Professor Crum—who hadn't? Hugo had read several of his books. He felt honored by the call and obligated to return it. He was curious as to why Professor Crum and not one of the students had telephoned him. Nevertheless, Hugo returned the call.

It was ten to five on November 6th when the phone rang at Duke University. Professor Crum answered the phone the way he usually did, "Crum, here."

Hugo introduced himself and said he was responding to the professor's Voicemail. The two chatted with Hugo complimenting the professor on his *Best Seller* books, and the professor reciprocated by complimenting Hugo on the popularity he had achieved with his well-written, well-expressed editorials. "So how can I help, Professor?" asked Hugo.

"Call me Eric," requested Professor Crum. "I would appreciate your helping a few of my students at Duke. I teach an advanced course on Political Science to seniors and grad students. They keep me on my toes. Well, this year we discussed the upcoming presidential election, the candidates, and what issues they thought the candidates should be addressing. Almost without exception, my students let me know they're not happy with any of the probable presidential party nominees. You have a few fans here at Duke, which leads me to my request. Several of my students would like to meet you and pick your brains."

Professor Crum knew that he was not being candid about the real reason the students wanted to meet Hugo. He knew he might be crossing the line, separating honesty and mild deception, but he thought in the end, Hugo would understand why a bit of deception was needed to lure him to agree to meet with his students.

"I'm flattered," said Hugo. "I never know how college students were reacting to what I say. I'd welcome the opportunity to share a few thoughts with your students. I'll find the time. I'll be going out of town for a few weeks but can meet when I return."

"You're making things easy for me, Hugo. I thought I would have to twist your arm. Thanks for being so gracious. I think you will enjoy a little give and take with this group. In fact, you might know one of them—Macey Lambert?"

"Mace—little Mace! I don't believe it. Why didn't he just call? The son of my boss—how could I refuse?"

"Well, you intimidate him, Hugo. He's a fine young man with lots of energy and ideas. He didn't want to contact you for fear you'd only agree to meet because of his father. You'll be impressed with this young man. And there are a couple of others in his group I think you will like—young and bright. They're our future leaders."

"Can they fly up here? If not, I will be in the North Carolina area in April. I could meet them then."

"How about on a Thursday, Friday, or Saturday? They said if I could set up a meeting, they'd be there. They could stay at Macey's family house in Chester. I understand that's not too far from you."

"It's the next town over." Hugo looked at his schedule. Then he said to Professor Crum, "Tell you what. I'll meet them at the Griswold Inn in Essex on Friday, November 10th. I'll arrange for lunch at noon and will stay as long as they would like. If that's OK with them, have Mace give me a call to confirm. I'm looking forward to seeing him as a young man."

CHAPTER 19

Bryan Center, Meeting Room B
11/7/2023

★ ★ ★

The Self Knowledge Symposium (SKS) meets weekly on Tuesdays at 7 p.m. in the Bryan Center on the West Campus of Duke University. Justin's dormitory was just a five-minute walk to the Center.

SKS, an educational, non-profit organization, is a resource for Duke students who are engaged in a spiritual search. The SKS community includes students, educators, alumni, and many others interested in spiritual seeking. Other chapters of SKS meet weekly on the campuses of North Carolina State and the University of North Carolina.

Tonight's meeting was to be a forum as part of the Interfaith Dialogue Project. The topic for this meeting was, "Searching for Truth Outside of Dogma: The SKS Approach to Spirituality." This particular forum was intended to be a continuation of the Duke effort to create dialogue about religious diversity.

Justin had been bothered ever since he left his meeting with Professor Ibala. When he was growing up in Pakistan, his life was programmed. Like many young Pakistani males, he was raised by Muslim parents in an Islamic religious environment, attended classes during the day, and played soccer after classes until prayer time. His

Muslin environment was the foundation for his learning and practicing Islam, a religion deeply rooted in the single belief and faith in one God (Allah), the belief that Muhammad was the last and most important of several prophets, and that the Quran was the last and final testament of Allah.

During prayer time, he would recite from the Quran in Arabic. Unlike many other young Muslims growing up in Pakistan, Justin's father influenced Justin to believe that the Quran called on all Muslims to oppose Christianity and Western society and culture, that Allah was the only recognized God, and that Islam was the chosen religion for all mankind. So that's what Justin believed when he began his college education at Duke.

Justin had a few non-Muslim friends at Duke. In fact, he was planning to meet one of his better friends, Blair Kurtz, at the Interfaith Dialogue forum. Blair, one of the fifteen students in Professor Crum's class, was a German-born American citizen who lived on Hilton Head Island in South Carolina. Justin and Blair had been friends since meeting on the soccer practice field during their sophomore years. They both played on Duke's 2022 soccer team, which finished the season with a record of thirteen wins, two losses, and four ties. The team finished first in the Coastal Division of the Atlantic Coast Conference.

Like Justin, Blair was a mid-fielder, though he spent most of the year on the sidelines on crutches with a broken ankle sustained during Duke's first soccer game of the season, a rout over Cornell. Justin and Blair were political science majors and often spent hours discussing politics and religion, sometimes heatedly. Both attended Duke's SKA meetings to better understand religious beliefs different from their own. Justin initially became involved with Duke's SKA at the suggestion of a Muslim acquaintance who wanted to make sure Islam was well-represented in the moral and spiritual discussions relating to religious diversity on campus.

The forum lasted from 7:30 until 9:45 p.m. There were eight panel members representing various religions and beliefs, including a catholic priest, a rabbi, and several protestant ministers from different sects, a Hindu graduate student, and a Durham High School teacher who also taught Islam at the Durham Islamic Center. The only member of the panel Justin recognized was Rawia Ismail, a teacher at the Islamic Center.

Each of the panelists made a presentation, followed by questions from an audience of over one hundred people. Blair always seemed to have a question for speakers. And tonight was no exception. He requested and was handed the microphone to ask the panel a question. "I'm not an Atheist," said Blair. "I do believe in a God, but I have a hard time understanding and accepting that God or Allah actually communicated directly with Moses and Mohammad or whomever, or that any such alleged communications or revelations were ever memorialized in religious works, such as the Bible, Quran, or Torah. Would any of you care to respond?"

The moderator was not prepared to have an open discussion on the authenticity of religious writings of various beliefs. He pre-empted any responses by saying that Blair's concerns were genuine, valid, and important, but responses from the panelists would take too much time, and perhaps might be a bit controversial—but would be an excellent topic for a discussion at a future forum when the panelists would have time to prepare for a discussion.

Justin did not ask any questions or make any comments. But he did appreciate the efforts by the panelists to hold open and frank discussions on aspects of religious beliefs too often not discussed or presented fairly and unbiased. As Blair and Justin left the auditorium,

Justin said to Blair, "You know, Blair, I'm a Muslim and have strong Muslim beliefs and ties. But you asked a good question tonight. I'd like to hear the answers. Just who and what were the influences behind the writings in the Bible or Quran or Torah?"

CHAPTER 20

Political Agenda of the Group of Five
11/8/2023

★ ★ ★

Macey, Blair, and Liz agreed to travel to Connecticut to meet Hugo on Friday, November 10th. Crystal and Justin had conflicts, but that was OK, as the feeling was that too many might be overpowering. They knew more than mild arm-twisting would be involved, and this might be their only shot at convincing Hugo to do something he was known to have said he would never do.

Nevertheless, all five were excited. Though chances of a third party winning the presidential election were remote, the Group was energized by the possibility that they could be instrumental in making changes to an election process that needed change. This was a chance to format future election practices so that voters would demand of politicians that they let the public know where they stood and what they would do with respect to critical matters important to our country and to the world. And this was an opportunity to have a presidential election that said, *No More,* to meaningless platitudes and empty promises.

Macey, Blair, and Liz agreed that the first item on their agenda for the meeting with Hugo was to satisfy themselves that Hugo was the person they deemed qualified to challenge the probable 2024 presidential nominees, Biden and Trump. If, after discussions with Hugo, the three agreed he was the one, the next agenda item was to let Hugo know they thought he would be a good choice for a third party run for the presidency. Then, assuming Hugo allowed discussions to proceed, the last agenda item, perhaps the most difficult to advance, was to convince him to put aside his private life in favor of pursuing a seemingly uphill battle to become the country's next president. "No easy task," said Macey, "but I think it's worth the effort."

The Group of Five was aware that fundraising would be crucial to Hugo if he decided to run. Blair volunteered to manage fund-raising. "I'll be prepared to discuss how the campaign would be funded. We won't do door-to-door knocking," said Blair, "because that would take too much time to raise the funds we'll need. Our fund-raising efforts can be put to better use through podcasts and video presentations placed on *social media*. Also, we will use choice placement of messages about the candidate on Google and other Internet *searching* sources. I've already established multiple websites to deliver messages in differing formats to our desired audience.

"The websites must be revised when and if we identify our candidate. These sites will allow us not only to do messaging, but also will serve as fund-raising vehicles.

"To broaden our audience, we'll use social media platforms like Twitter, Facebook, TikTok, and YouTube. I'm sure we'll be able to attract several interested techies to assist in the use of these sources. I'm not a Techie, but once we announce the campaign, we should have no problem retaining technical students from Duke and other schools to staff whatever we need to do. We'll encourage the first wave of staffers to invite all their friends and their friend's friends to participate in the process."

Liz and Crystal previously had volunteered to handle the staffing for the campaign. They had no experience in campaign staffing, but they were neither dummies nor shy. Liz told them that she and Crystal would generate a list of volunteers from all the states. "This shouldn't be hard. There's plenty of dissatisfaction out there. We can develop a staff network through use of social media platforms and email messaging."

"How will you interest volunteers?" asked Blair.

"We won't beat around the bush. Our message will be clear. We'll tell them we're not happy with the candidates running for presidency. Therefore, we're soliciting anyone with an interest in becoming involved in backing a person better qualified and with more substance. We'll tell them we're putting together a team to propose an alternative to the present candidates, and that we have identified the ideal person. If we are successful in convincing that person to run, he'll be our man."

"Ideally," said Macey, "we'll need well-staffed organizations in all states. And we'll have to rely on these organizations for requesting contributions and for message networking. Once we start receiving campaign funds, we'll pay for some expertise. In the meantime, we're it!"

CHAPTER 21

Flight 4663 to Connecticut
11/9/2023

American Airlines Flight 4663 left Raleigh-Durham International Airport at 9:55 a.m. and arrived at Bradley International Airport on time at 11:30 am, a one hour and thirty-five-minute flight. Bradley International Airport is located within the towns of Windsor Locks, Suffield and East Granby, Connecticut, about halfway between Hartford, Connecticut and Springfield, Massachusetts. The ride to Chester, Connecticut was no more than an hour from the airport … traffic permitting. Macey lived with his parents in a white Cape Cod style house on 28 Liberty Street in Chester.

Chester is a small New England town located on the Connecticut River. Now it has quaint shops, art galleries, upscale specialty shops, a number of small restaurants and pubs that attract tourists, a fire department and one of the oldest fife and drum corps in the state. Seventy years ago, it was a sleepy town with about 3,000 residents, several small manufacturing plants, a rough and tumble pub, a liquor store, an ice cream parlor, and several specialty stores where residents could purchase necessities.

Over time the factories closed, older families moved on, houses were restored or torn down and replaced, real estate prices soared, and the town, though still small in numbers, no longer is considered a sleepy Connecticut River oriented town. Macey's family purchased the home they now reside in from 5th generation members of the Brooks family, a family that owned a nearby metal parts business established in 1847.

Macey introduced Blair and Liz to his parents. His parents were aware Macey would be bringing a couple of classmates. They knew the three of them would be meeting with Hugo the next day at the Griswold Inn. But they didn't know why. Macey went out of his way not to get his father involved.

Macey's mother, Leona, didn't like to cook. She liked to play golf, travel, shop, antique, and a few other things, but not cook. So that's why she invited Macey and his friends out to dinner that night.

"How about The Copper Beech Inn? Do you think your guests would like that, Mace?" Leona Lambert liked The Copper Beech Inn. It was nearby, a bit pricy, but you must wear a jacket. It was considered by locals to be a Four-Diamond AAA rated restaurant. A few years ago, the Inn was one of the top 100 hotel restaurants in America by USA Today. For all the same reasons, Jack Lambert preferred to go elsewhere.

Macey saved his father from asserting an opinion. "I don't dress up, Mom. It's too fancy there. Isn't there a pub where we can get a sandwich and beer?" Macey had been to The Copper Beech Inn with his parents several times before. A Navy-Blue blazer, khaki pants, Brooks Brother's buttoned-down blue shirt was acceptable garb. Macey knew this wouldn't go over with Blair and Liz. That's not what he wanted either.

So as a compromise and at the suggestion of Leona, it was agreed that dinner would be at the Brasserie Pub, the more casual dining area within The Copper Beech Inn. Jackets and ties were not required, and dressy casual was OK. But no jeans. Leona also liked it there because not long-ago readers of Connecticut Magazine rated the pub one of the best casual restaurants along the shoreline.

Dinner was pleasant. Everyone got along. Mom Lambert, though somewhat pompous when it came to dining, enjoyed a better relationship with her son than her husband did. She would do whatever for Macey to make him happy. She was an extrovert, intelligent, and could talk on any level on almost any topic. And she knew when to shut her mouth.

Macey's Dad was different. He was more controlling and always wanted to know what Macey was doing and thinking. Macey and his dad often didn't see eye to eye. That's the reason Macey didn't reveal to his parents the real purpose of his meeting with Hugo.

After dinner Pop pried a bit. "So, what's the big meeting about tomorrow? You want to go into the newspaper business? If so, Hugo can give you a few good tips."

"Don't think so, Dad. Mr. McCormick is an interesting person. Lots of good ideas. We're working on a class project. Just want to pick his brain."

The Griswold Inn

CHAPTER 22

The Griswold Inn,
Lunch with Hugo
11/10/2023

★ ★ ★

The Griswold Inn is in Essex, Connecticut. In continuous operation since being built in 1776, the Inn consists of the main house and seven other buildings constituting the Griswold Inn Campus. All the guestrooms were refurbished recently, retaining a colonial décor, but upgraded with modern necessities—still no televisions. According to the owners, the Paul brothers and families, you don't go to Essex or The Griswold Inn to watch TV.

The Inn had four main dining rooms, one with a collection of antique guns on the walls, appropriately named the Gun Room. Hanging on the walls of the three other dining rooms could be found a collection of maritime art, one of the largest in the country.

Just before the entrance to the main dining room was a small but active tap room with an iron pot-bellied stove in the center of the room, an antique popcorn maker next to an old but well maintained piano, and hard oakwood chairs not designed for comfortable sitting. The tap room is known throughout the state as a jovial place to congregate and listen on any given night to banjo, jazz, Dixieland, rock, or sea chantey music between the hours of 7:30 to 12:00 midnight. Lunch was served in the tap room from 11 am to 5 pm where diners could order lunch from a wide selection of items described on a menu entitled Tavern Fare.

When Hugo was courting Louise and a few years thereafter, the two often would dine at the Inn, particularly choosing a Friday or Saturday evening when they could expect to be entertained by John Banker, a charismatic musical personality. Although he had a small band called Riverboat Ramblers, he often performed solo with audience participation doing specialty programs with nostalgia, humor and lots of showmanship. Banker could play all sorts of musical instruments, many, such as his washboard, not identifiable as sophisticated musical instruments. After dinner, Louise and Hugo joined in with the singing crowd, and Louise, after a couple of glasses of wine at dinner, to the enjoyment of other patrons, often and at the right moment in a tune, rang the huge clanging bell hanging on one of the tap room walls.

Lunch at the Inn on a Friday in November normally isn't busy. Hugo reserved a table in the Covered Bridge section of the main dining room, an area partially constructed with remnants of an old, abandoned bridge from New Hampshire.

Shortly before 12 noon, Macey, Blair and Liz stood at the entrance of the tap room looking down and around to see if they could spot Hugo from pictures they had googled. He wasn't hard to spot among the three patrons standing at the bar. Though not a beer drinker, Hugo enjoyed a dirty vodka martini when he was in the mood. He was in the mood that day as he stood having his favorite drink while waiting for his guests. From the end of the bar, he spotted the three peering down from the steps leading into the bar area, and assumed they were Macey and his friends. Hugo signaled to them with his right index finger that he was the one for whom they were looking.

'"Now you must be Mace," Hugo said. "You look like your father —well not exactly. You're a few years younger and a few pounds lighter. And your dad has decided he looks more distinguished wearing a grayish, Lincoln style Beard."

"That's me, Mr. McCormick," said Macey. " I'm the little kid you met a few years ago. Yup! My father thinks he's the hometown Santa Clause. He has worn a beard since last Christmas. Thanks for agreeing to meet with us."

"My pleasure," said Hugo. "But no more Mr. McCormick. Call me Hugo. That's what I like to be called. You guys are college graduates now—or almost, and you're now at least my equal. So, it's first names. OK."

The three smiled and nodded OK, acknowledging but not accepting that they were now Hugos equal. "These are my friends from Duke," said Macey —"Liz Reicher and Blair Kurtz. We're seniors and working on a class project."

"Great,' said Hugo. "Hope I can help. I reserved a table in the other room. We should be able to talk there."

The table in the Covered Bridge section of the main dining room was situated against two wood paneled walls to the right and rear of their table. Hugo had asked the maître d' if he would leave the table next to them empty as Hugo wanted privacy. "No problem, Mr. McCormick. We don't expect a large lunch crowd today."

Next, the waiter came, recited the lunch specials, then took the drink orders. Macey and Liz ordered ice tea, Blair ordered a Virgin Mary. Hugo ordered another dirty vodka martini on the rocks. Two was his limit. Three and he might start doing and saying things he shouldn't.

"So, Mace, what do you want to talk about? Your father told me you and your friends might want to get into the newspaper business. If so, you're talking to the wrong guy."

Macey shook his head from side to side. As the anointed speaker, he told Hugo that the three were interested in the next presidential election. Tainted with a little white lie, Macey said he and his friends were involved in a class project to prepare a paper on the presidential candidates, who are the best qualified, and why.

He went on to say they were familiar with Hugo from his editorials, liked what he had to say, and wanted to pick his brains on a few of the more important issues the presidential candidates should be talking about, but don't.

"Shoot," said Hugo. "I'm glad to meet a few people who read my editorials."

The three students looked at each other with facial expressions suggesting a better than average start. Hugo was willing to talk about anything.

Macey continued, "Well, we're concerned that what we see as the critical problems facing the United States are not being addressed by any of the presidential contenders. What's worse is that the critical problems not being addressed are not even being identified as problems. For instance, what will the President or Congress do to encourage a cultural change so that our country doesn't always have to defend against acts of terrorism or war?

"We think too many countries clash with each other over differences which should be resolved short of war. Why can't countries look beyond our cultural differences and beliefs and recognize world peace and the existence of mankind are the bigger issues with which we *should* be concerned. So, if you don't mind, Hugo, we'd like to hear your thoughts on world peace, and whether you think we are mere dreamers. Should we stop dreaming and accept that world peace will never see existence."

"Wow! I didn't see that coming," said Hugo with his chin resting in the palm of his right hand, "but a good inquiry. You might not be aware, but I recently finished writing a book which included my views on this very same topic. The book is called *No More Small Talk*.

"One of the chapters discusses my thoughts on pursuing a realistic approach to a world where wars no longer have significance. It's an objective that won't be resolved overnight, and will never result unless world peace is recognized by the major powers as essential in order to prepare against any global catastrophes which someday might threaten life on our planet. I have copies of my book in my car. When we leave, I'll give you copies.

"Here's my thoughts in a nutshell: two long term, well entrenched beliefs need to change if ever we are to experience living in a world without wars. **One** is that non-consensual territorial expansion by countries through acts of war needs to cease. And **two**, diverse religious differences among religious groups worldwide, like those who believe in Christianity, Judaism, Islam or whatever, need to be acknowledged, respected, and tolerated by all religious groups."

"Would you elaborate," said Blair. "Do you think Biden or Trump or any of the other candidates would ever consider events which might jeopardize life on Earth?"

"Fair point, Blair," said Hugo. "I doubt it. But think about it—human existence on Earth is not a given. There are too many threats to our planet which can only be effectively addressed by the joint efforts of the leaders of the powerful countries. For example, what would happen if our planet collided with a huge asteroid or other Earth-shattering object? Or people or things from other planets suddenly appeared at our doorsteps? Or the Sun no longer is capable of being our primary source of heat and light? Or an uncontrollable deadly infectious disease spread globally so that the disease wiped out all or most of mankind? Or how would the United States be affected if the space above Earth becomes exclusively controlled by a foreign country, like China or Russia—or worse, by inhabitants of another planet?

"Perhaps mankind's biggest threat today is full-blown nuclear war with unmeasurable catastrophic consequences. Doesn't territorial grabbing through force become unimportant when compared to a catastrophic event that could wipe out mankind? We need the leaders of our more powerful nations to work together to manage catastrophic threats, rather than clash with others over relatively less important differences."

"I don't want to appear cynical," said Blair, "but don't you think changing long term, well-settled views on territorial borders is close to impossible?"

"No, I don't think so," answered Hugo. "But again, the leaders of the major powers, including the United States, China, Russia, North Korea, Israel and Palestine, need to recognize that in order to protect mankind from threats of catastrophic events, joint action by all countries is a must. However, joint action will never happen unless wars among countries cease."

Liz nodded in general agreement with what Hugo was saying. *No more small talk* thought Liz to herself. I think I might like this guy.

After lunch the plates were cleared. Hugo and Blair ordered coffee. Lis and Macey ordered another iced tea.

"Mr. McCormick," said Liz. "I read an article you recently wrote on income inequality. My recollection is that you said narrowing the gap between income groups could favorably influence existing problems with health care, gangs, drugs, crime, and other social issues. Could you be more specific?"

"I remember the article, Liz," said Hugo. "I define income inequality as the extent to which income is distributed unevenly among a population. Clearly many persons receive incomes far greater than what is reasonably necessary to reward motivation, skill, talent, leadership, and entrepreneurship. On the other extreme, too many hard-working persons, for whatever reason, never will be able to earn enough to rise above poverty level. In my view, this gross disparity should not be a liberal and conservative battleground. Simply put, some people make too little. Some people make too much."

"So, what's wrong with that," said Blair. "How much is too much?"

"What's enough? I don't know," said Hugo. "I'd say net earnings of up to thirty million dollars a year is more than sufficient to fuel the motivational incentives of persons living in a free and capitalistic society.

"Does a person need an income greater than that to motivate drive and ambition? What does an executive or entertainer or professional athlete do to demand an income four to five hundred times more than a policeman, a fireman or a teacher? In the long run, if we're going to preserve our capitalistic way of life here in the States, our financial reward system had better change so that people at the bottom can be motivated to perform equally as much as people at the top."

"Sounds like creeping socialism," said Blair. "So, what would you propose if you were president?"

"I don't have all the answers" said Hugo. "Income inequality should be one of the defining issues of the upcoming presidential election. A competitive, capitalistic free enterprise society needs a financial system that not only motivates advantaged persons but also motivates and rewards performance by hard working, low income disadvantaged persons. I think rather than income equality, income insufficiency better defines the income gap. This is not socialism. I'd call it ratcheting our society to raise the spending power of lower paid persons to levels which would permit them to live a better life, resulting in a reduction in the number of persons needing entitlements, and the reduction of those who are tempted to engage in stealing or dealing in drugs to put food on the table."

"But you haven't answered my question." responded Blair.

"No, I haven't, have I," said Hugo. "Well, let me give you an answer. If I were president, I'd acknowledge changes must be made to reduce the number of persons relying on or taking advantage of our entitlement programs. I would persuade members of Congress to take politics out of the equation in addressing income inequality. I would establish a committee of social and economic thinkers, not politicians and not necessarily economists, but a mixture of liberals, conservatives, and persons in between who are capable of evaluating problems and issues in a bi-partisan manner.

"The committee's objective would be to put together a proposal and eventual plan for reducing the number of have-nots in our society. My guidance to the committee would be to consider revising the tax code so that anyone with a net income of under $150,000 would pay no income tax, those with net incomes between $150,000 to $30,000,000 would pay income taxes, and at the existing rates. Any net income earned by individuals or households in excess of $30,000,000 would be taxed at a rate of 85%, maybe more.

"The precise amounts for each category can be the subject of discussion and negotiation. The higher taxes paid on excessive net incomes would offset the loss of tax revenues on incomes of less than $150,000. The bottom line is that persons or households earning less than $150,000 would be retaining more of their income, while persons with net incomes more than $30,000,000 would be encouraged by the high tax rates to reduce their financial expectations and demands. Over time, such a plan will ultimately result in a cultural change whereby employment contracts for excessive incomes will no longer be sought or demanded, and the monies not paid to excessive income generators would be used by businesses to pay higher incomes and benefits to lower paid workers."

"Do you really think such a change in our tax code stands a chance? said Blair.

"If members of Congress work together, why wouldn't it? A better question is what will happen if we don't put more money in the pockets of lower income earners? If we don't prioritize finding ways to provide more spending power to those in the lower income brackets, thus enabling them to buy a house, a car, eat three meals a day or enjoy a few of the amenities others enjoy, then we are sitting on a time bomb—setting the stage for eventual strikes, riots, and other acts of violence by those seeking a better life."

"Why don't any of the presidential candidates share your views?" said Liz.

"I think most do," said Hugo, "but don't want to say so for fear of losing votes. My thinking is that such changes in our tax structure are not socialism at work, but, rather, an effort to take our capitalistic-based, free enterprise system to a better level."

"So, Hugo," said Macey, "it appears you think the presidential candidates are ducking what you consider important presidential considerations. Who do you intend to vote for in November?"

"Who would I vote for?" said Hugo. "I assume you mean for the presidency. Right now, I wouldn't vote for any of the candidates, certainly not Biden or Trump. I don't know what any of the candidates think about the things I believe are important. But I'm not voting for a person if the only thing I know about him or her is the name of the party with which they are affiliated. Others might vote along party lines, but I won't. It's a shame too many voters routinely vote the party line or vote for a candidate simply because what a candidate might say on a particular issue—like abortion, gay rights or gun control—totally ignoring what that candidate might say or do on more important issues. I'll continue expressing my thoughts on what the candidates do or don't do in my editorials."

Hugo paused for a moment—then excused himself to go the men's room. "I'll be back. You guys ever take a pee break?"

The students also had to go but needed a few moments without Hugo to decide what's next. "He gets a thumbs up from me." said Macey. Blair and Liz nodded their heads in agreement. "Now where do we go from here?" said Liz.

They all knew what's next. Hugo had no idea that three young college students were thinking about asking him to consider running for the presidency. Hugo had been flattered to have been asked by Professor Crum to meet with his students, and he was flattered that Macey and a couple of his Duke friends would make the trip from Durham, North Carolina to ask him questions when they could have read his book. Hugo certainly didn't expect that soon they would be asking him to run against the probable major party nominees, Biden and Trump, for president of the United States.

The men's room was near the tap room, a short distance away. Hugo peed, washed his hands, and returned within five minutes. "Are we about finished? You asked some good questions. I'm glad to see Duke taught you how to think."

"Almost," said Macey while staring into Hugo's eyes, "but we have just one more item. Could you tell us three good reasons why you wouldn't consider running for the presidency?"

Hugo, looking somewhat perplexed, replied ''Me! Are you kidding? You want only three reasons?"

"No. Seriously," said Macey. ''If someone were to ask you to run, what would you say?"

Hugo didn't know where this conversation was going. He suspected he had to carefully craft a response as he was beginning to sense that these three college students had a different agenda than what he was led to believe. He considered dismissing the whole subject by laughing and making light of the question, but he didn't want to insult Macey and his friends. So, he responded.

"I had my run at politics. It was not a pleasant experience, and I have no desire to get involved again, ever. I enjoy what I'm doing. I believe I can be more effective as a political pundit where I'm able to pressure legislators to act on matters politicians prefer to ignore. Perhaps the most important reason I wouldn't run is that my wife will probably divorce me if I even mention the thought of returning to politics."

Hugo looked at three disappointed faces—all with deep frown lines. "And let's not overlook the practical aspects of challenging the other candidates. Not only is it too late to enter the race, but the probable major party nominees, Biden and Trump, have been running for over a year. They have war chests that could bury new opponents."

Blair didn't like the negative thoughts coming out of Hugo's mouth. He also was a bit upset that with so much at stake, Hugo was showing signs of being someone resigned to accept one of two poor choices as the next president.

At the risk of infuriating Hugo, Blair responded to Hugo "Bull— you talk a good game in your editorials, so why not act rather than pen a few words? You haven't given us one good reason why you shouldn't run. You only have given us *excuses* as to why you won't run."

Macey, a shade more diplomatic than Blair, decided he had better step in before Hugo became upset and left. "I guess we've been dishonest with you Hugo. I'll take the blame. Now I'll level with you."

Macey told Hugo that he, Blair, and Liz had just completed an advanced political science course at Duke. He said the course was not just a typical course, but a much in-demand course taught by Professor Crum. Professor Crum had assigned the class a project to identify and evaluate the important social, economic, and political issues that the next administration should address—and then discuss how we thought each of the candidates were addressing those issues. "We had no problem identifying and prioritizing important issues. But we did have a problem recognizing how the candidates were addressing the issues. Surprisingly, what we considered important issues were not even discussed by any of the candidates. Lots of personal attacks, lots of promises, lots of empty rhetoric, and lots of criticisms of each other. Not one candidate dared stake a position on issues we thought should be discussed.

"On the last day of class, Professor Crum took a poll to see how each of us would vote in the next presidential election. Out of 15 persons in the class, two didn't have an opinion, and the rest voted for none of the above."

"I'm following so far," said Hugo. "So, why are we here?"

Macey continued by telling Hugo that on the last day of class, Professor Crum challenged the class to stay involved in the political process if we weren't satisfied with the choice of presidential candidates. He told us we were the future generation, and if we didn't like what's going on in this world, we should not complain, stop being wimps—and do something about it. He didn't say what to do, but you could sense he would be disappointed if we did nothing. So, a few days after the course ended, several of us decided to meet on a casual basis and, if nothing more, hash out a few things which weren't resolved in class. "That's where you came in."

"Me! How do I fit in?" said Hugo.

Macey told Hugo he and several others were disappointed with the pool of candidates who announced intentions to run for the presidency, and it looked like the voters again would have to choose a president not deserving of the office. ''So,'' said Macey ''we decided to search for a person more deserving of the office, a person with name recognition, a person with vision for what's best for our country, and a person who would pursue changes so that partisan politics would not continue to be the impediment now crippling routine Congressional performance. We sifted through a long list of names—and your name came to the top of the pile. We would like you to run."

Hugo couldn't believe what he just heard. He thought he was meeting with a bunch of college kids to pick his brains about journalism and writing editorials on matters which affect our country and way of life. It never occurred to him that these same kids would be asking him to run for the presidency. He sensed they were serious, as they anxiously awaited a response. They saw something in Hugo that Hugo didn't see in himself.

"Even if I said Yes," said Hugo, ''How could this ever be pulled off? I like the way you're thinking, but it's too late in the game. Besides, the two major parties have all but selected who they want as their nominees."

"Will you run if we can convince you it's not too late?" said Macey. "We don't think it is. We've done our homework. We've tested the waters. We think you could win."

Hugo sat quietly at the table. He was thinking. After a few moments of silence, Hugo said "I'll hear you out. Convince me it's not too late."

It was quarter to four. The three students reached first base. Macey, Blair, and Liz had a game plan, but needed more time to prepare a convincing argument. Macey asked Hugo if he had time tomorrow to listen to their plan.

Hugo said he'd like to give this more thought, and that he would discuss the proposal with Louise.

They agreed to meet tomorrow at one o'clock at Hugo's house. Hugo gave them directions. The three students left the Inn, stopping at Hugo's car so they could obtain copies of his book.

CHAPTER 23

Back to Chester after the Meeting
11/10/2023

When they arrived at the Inn on Friday at noon, the sky was overcast and the temperature a chilly thirty-three degrees. When they had left, it was snowing—not an unusual event in Essex at this time of the year. The black Lexus SUV they had rented was covered with a thin layer of fine snow. After cleaning off the windshields, the three began the short trip back to Chester.

Macey thought he would spend a few more days with his parents. Blair and Liz had planned to return to Durham after the meeting with Hugo. But there was still work to be done, so Liz and Blair changed their return flight to Sunday morning.

The trip to Chester from the Griswold Inn gave them time to discuss what to say to Hugo on Saturday. They agreed Hugo would have to be convinced he would have a credible chance of winning. He also had to be convinced that a plan was in place to jumpstart Hugo's late entry into the campaign, that funding would not be a significant issue, a talented election team would be put in place immediately, a new party entity would be established, and all the necessary filings and paperwork would be done so that his name would appear on all state election ballots.

The Group of Five already had begun preliminary preparations for a possible third-party candidacy before Macey, Blair and Liz departed Durham.

Macey agreed to put together a plan for discussing Saturday's meeting with Hugo. Prior to traveling to Connecticut, Macey asked Justin to research dormant registered party organizations with the thought of piggybacking onto an organization already in existence. They were aware that the political philosophy of the assumed organization would have to be abandoned and reconstituted with a new organizational structure and political platform.

Macey said he would develop a proposed platform of issues and ideas, recognizing that Hugo would have the final say—if he decided to run. Blair was prepared to comment on campaign funding, and Liz said she would take on the responsibility of putting together an organizational chart with the names and duties of staffers willing to assist in campaign funding, planning, and coordinating campaign activities.

"I have a proposed campaign plan on my word processor," said Macey, "but I'll need your help with details by tonight. This is it! We need to convince Hugo we're organized."

CHAPTER 24

Justin's Dorm at Duke
11/10/2023

★ ★ ★

It was 7:25 Friday evening when Justin's cell phone rang. He was in his dorm room, propped against a pillow with a book opened, but eyes shut. He had too much on his mind to find room in his brain to digest what he was attempting to read.

The phone call was from Macey, giving him an update on his meeting with Hugo and checking to see if he had a chance to dig up information on dormant political organizations that could be used for an entry into the presidential race. Macey told Justin that they were meeting with Hugo again tomorrow, hoping to convince him to run. "Fifty-fifty chance," said Macey, "but we'll need to show him we're ready to support him if he'll run."

After briefly discussing the formation of a new party, Justin said, "I googled the *Net* yesterday and found there are about a hundred political organizations that are registered but now are dormant. I contacted the owners of three of them.

There's one organization that was registered, but never advanced beyond that. I spoke to one of the listed founders to see if we could purchase the party name. Without mentioning specific persons, I revealed the political philosophies and ideas of the candidate we would be backing. This person didn't want to get involved but said the founders would assign its party name to us along with all registered rights, in exchange for one thousand dollars and the execution of a release for all future liability resulting from our use of the name. This might just work for us. The name of the party is Practical Party of the People. What do you think? Does it sound too socialistic?"

Macey asked Justin to follow up and keep them interested in selling—and do whatever paperwork is necessary to purchase the rights to the name. "If Hugo says he'll run, I'll ask one of my friends at the law school to help with acquiring the registered entity. We have the meeting with Hugo on Saturday, but I'll be back in Durham on Tuesday. See you then."

Justin remained on his bed after the phone call. He wanted to continue to be part of the Group of Five and was looking forward to being involved in a hands-on effort to elect the next president. But his allegiance to his faith was tested when he was requested by Malcolm earlier in the day to attend a meeting on November 12th in Raleigh with Professor Ibala and several others.

"We need your attendance," said Malcolm. "Something has come up and Professor Ibala thinks you could help. He wouldn't say how."

More and more Justin was beginning to feel the pressure of being pulled in two different directions by compelling sources. He was well aware he was in way over his head with Professor Ibala, Malcolm, and whoever else was part of any radical Islamic plans. They were the ones who supported him and his Islamic values for four years as a student at Duke.

And yet he didn't want to forfeit his position as a member of the Group of Five as he had the rare opportunity of being the only Muslim in a non-Muslim environment, accepted by Christians and Jews to participate in the possible election of the next president of the United States.

CHAPTER 25

Hugo's House - Mack Lane, Essex
11/11/2023

The trip from Liberty Street in Chester to 120 Mack Lane in Essex took 20 minutes. The snow had stopped, and the accumulation was insignificant. The temperature was in the mid-thirties. Hugo lived at the corner of the street, just before the bend to the right. His house was a blue and gray, three story, colonial house overlooking Middle Harbor. It was one o'clock when they arrived. Hugo had been expecting them. The house was empty except for Hugo. Hugo's wife planned a hairdresser's appointment at one, thereby giving Hugo exclusive use of the house.

Hugo offered his guests a soft drink before going into the living room. Macey and Liz had diet cokes, Blair a glass of ice water. They sat down in swivel chairs and an oversized circular sofa in front of a large flagstone fireplace with a glowing fire.

Hugo moved right to the purpose of the meeting. He said, "I discussed our conversation with my wife. She didn't get completely turned off by the thought of me running for president, but thought I was hanging around with some pretty nutty persons."

Macey, who stayed up most of the night preparing for the meeting, handed Hugo a five-page summary of how the campaign would proceed, provided he decided to run.

Hugo briefly looked over the summary. "I'm impressed. You've done your homework." said Hugo. "I wouldn't have invited you here if I didn't want to hear more about your proposal. So convince me why I should run. Running for the presidency cost money—lots of money!"

"We agree. Funding is critical," responded Macey. And Blair will be the point person on funding." Macey nodded to Blair to brief Hugo on how funding would be handled.

Blair then took over the discussion. "We conducted preliminary polls through use of several websites we've already established and through use of a few You-Tube videos. We found there are lots of younger generation voters, mostly college students, who are dissatisfied with either Biden or Trump being our next president. We plan to recruit a number of those dissatisfied to assist in fund-raising efforts and to staff our campaign operations.

"Liz and Crystal had already begun the process of setting up funding organizations in each state. A copy of our proposed fund-raising organizational structure is attached to the summary Macey gave you. If you say you will run, we will begin fund raising immediately. All we will need is your input for the videos, including a definitive statement setting forth the reasons why you're running.

"I'll set up fund accounts so we comply with all federal funding reporting requirements. Liz and Crystal already have enlisted a few other geek type persons who will assist in advertising and marketing. Liz, maybe you should comment on what you have done so far?"

"Be glad to," said Liz. "Not knowing whether you would or wouldn't run, but for planning purposes, we just assumed you would. We'll need pictures, videos, and a list of reasons why you'll be running. Then we'll put this information on our websites and on social networks. We'll use search vehicles, like Goggle, positioning information about you and your campaign. That way, anytime persons searching for news relating to the presidential election will be referred to our pre-established sites. Our websites and messages will be the first listing. We will do the same with professional networking sites like www.linkedin.com, www.zoominfo.com, www.naymz.com and www.spoke.com."

"Looks like your plan is to run a high-tech campaign," said Hugo. "How would you get the press to support me?"

"We thought of that," answered Macey. "We plan to take the campaign directly to the people. Since much of the so-called free press is biased in favor of Biden or Trump, soliciting its support at this time might be counterproductive. But we don't want to ignore the press. They can be a powerful adversary. We won't shun them, but we plan to dance around them by internet campaigning and online town hall meetings. We'll handle the mechanics of all that. Leave that to us geeks.

"Once campaign funds become available, we will be placing newspaper and TV advertisements highlighting your platform with bullet point issues and proposals. We'll supply our staffers with brochures explaining in clear and simple language who you are, why you're running, and what you'll do when elected. Everything will be communicated in clear and simple questions and answers format. We will begin orchestrating a series of personal appearances which we feel you should make in major cities throughout the states. We can always fine tune campaign plans along the way. What do you think?"

"I have a small problem," said Hugo. "I would be going from a person with a modest paying job to a person who is unemployed. I don't think I can afford that."

"We thought of that also," said Macey. "I talked to my Dad last night. I told him what we were doing, including trying to convince you to run for the presidency. He was shocked—but after giving it some thought said 'great'. He even told me he'd give you a paid leave of absence until after the election. I think he believes his paper would reap benefits from your becoming a presidential candidate. Whatever, he's all for your running.

"And if you decide to run, our team will be at your disposal. There are five of us who formed the initial team. We refer to ourselves as the Group of Five. And we have many followers and friends just waiting to help. Granted we are not professionals, and we might be a little rough around the edges, but we do get things done."

Hugo sat back in his chair, clasped his hands in front of him, looked at Macey, Liz and Blair and said, "When do you want an answer?"

"Right now," said Macey. "There's nothing more we can add. We think you're the person we've been seeking. We're prepared to pull the switch. If you say no, we're out of here. No questions asked."

Appearing as though he had already made up his mind before the meeting, Hugo responded, "Then let's go for it, Group of Five! I couldn't ask for a better team. I'm not saying yes just to muddy the waters. I'm in it to win. However, I must insist on a few basic things, such as no negative campaigning. My message to the people is to be simple and clear, and I'll run on a platform that has only six or seven national and global issues important to me and to the public. I will not mince words when expressing my thoughts and opinions.

"One last thing," Hugo said in a voice that left no uncertainty as to who would be in charge. "Our slogan for the campaign will be the same as the title of my book: *No More Small Talk*."

CHAPTER 26

Campaign Strategy Meeting
11/12/2023

It was Sunday morning. Macey's father was sitting in the kitchen having a light breakfast with Macey and his friends. Liz and Blair already had packed. They were taking a 1:20 pm flight back to Durham --- planning to leave Chester for Bradley International Airport by 11:00. Jack could sense the excitement among the three as they revealed their efforts to have Hugo elected president. There was much work left to be done. They seemed to ignore that the responsibilities of running a campaign might conflict with graduating from Duke next year.

Macey planned to return to Durham on Tuesday. While still in Connecticut, he wanted to take pictures of Hugo and his wife for brochures for Hugo's campaign. And he wanted to assist in formalizing and publicizing the platform Hugo would soon make known to the public.

Before leaving to return to Durham, Blair told Macey he'd immediately jump-start the process of campaign funding, BUT that he'd hold off until brochures with Hugo's platform and campaign pictures could be printed. "This will be a grass roots campaign," said Blair. "I'll work closely with Liz and Crystal to coordinate funding."

Macey had made plans to spend most of Sunday afternoon with Hugo. When he arrived at Hugo's house, he met Hugo's wife for the first time. "So, you're Macey," said Louise. "Thanks a lot. I leave Hugo alone for a few minutes and the next thing I know, he's running for president." Louise sounded like she was complaining, but she knew how elated her husband was by having the opportunity to do something in Washington he was unable to do before.

Hugo and Macey got right down to business. Macey used his smart phone to take pictures of Hugo sitting at his desk, drinking coffee on the porch, leaning on the backyard picket fence, and sitting at the breakfast table with Louise. Macey planned to match the pictures with campaign slogans and statements he would soon be obtaining from Hugo. Louise excused herself from their presence and went to the sun porch, a room adjacent to the kitchen. When she left, Macey couldn't help noticing that Louise was carrying a cane in her left hand and walked with a noticeable limp which she modestly attempted to conceal, but couldn't.

When Macey had enough pictures, he and Hugo sat and talked. Hugo, referring to notes he had scribbled earlier in the day on the back of a white, blank envelope, was anxious to set forth his version of how his campaign should proceed. "Let's start with campaign issues and promises. We discussed most at lunch on Friday. But important things are worth repeating. I recognize there will be persons with different views than what I'll be saying, particularly Biden, Trump, and their followers. So, let's be clear, let them be critical—and regardless what they say about me, I will not engage in a negative campaign, and I won't encourage false news about my opponents be put out by our campaign staff—that's just not my style."

Hugo listed *World Peace* as one of the six platform concerns with which he would focus. Hugo wanted Macey and the Group of Five to know his thinking on World Peace. So, he told Macey he believed ending the present conflict in the Mideast between the Israelis and the

Palestinians would be a giant step toward World Peace. "I recognize the struggle of Palestinians and Israelis to establish homelands in the lands both now occupy has been going on for years if not centuries, but the fighting needs to cease if world peace is to be achieved. And we'll never see World Peace if radical Islamic jihadists continue to spread the notion that exclusive Islamic religious views ultimately will rule the world. How will we ever find a path to world peace when a few Islamic leaders continuously call for the death of the American and Israeli people?" Hugo said, if elected, he would encourage discussions with leaders of the more powerful countries to recognize that catastrophic events which threaten the existence of human life on our planet can only be prevented if countries jointly work together in an environment of global peace.

Then Hugo said, "**Income Disparity** also needs to be a platform issue. We need to come to grips with the gross disparity among income levels of the rich and poor in the United States—and abroad. It's not so much the disparities in incomes between the *haves* and the *have nots,* but the insufficiency of incomes of those in poverty or near poverty level. I don't see an easy fix, but a change in our tax rates which would put more money in the pockets of the *have nots* might be a solution. I envision a plan where net incomes below a certain level, say $150,000, would be tax exempt. Then, more persons would have additional disposal income in their pockets. The more people financially able to afford household expenses, private health care plans, and education tuition, the fewer who will need government assistance from entitlement programs."

"So, what will we call this platform issue?" said Macey. "Income inequality?"

"We'll label it such for the platform," said Hugo. But in reality it should be called **Tax Relief for Lower Income Persons**."

Another issue Hugo wanted to insert into his platform related to the increase of drug related crimes. "There has been a dramatic increase in crimes and the number and size of transnational street gangs during the past five years," said Hugo. "And the selling of illegal drugs is a pivotal contributor to the increase." In Hugo's opinion, unemployment and low paying jobs made dealing in illegal drugs an attractive side business—notwithstanding the risks of being caught.

"So your solution is what?" said Macey.

"Legalize the sale and use of drugs to anyone over eighteen," said Hugo. "Are you with me on this Mace?" Hugo asked.

"I guess!" said Macey. "You're going to open lots of mouths. So, will legalization of drugs be a platform issue?"

"No. Let's call it **Reducing crimes in America,**" said Hugo. "I suspect if we just say legalization of drugs, the whole point for legalizing drugs might be lost. I realize I'll need to convince persons with different views that controlled legalization of drugs in the long run would be best for our country."

"What about **Immigration** as another platform issue?" said Macey, not wanting to engage Hugo on the pros and cons of legalizing drugs.

"You're jumping ahead of me, Mace. But I agree. We need laws which prohibit entrance into our country of all persons not legally entitled to be here. No exceptions. And we need to strictly enforce these laws. Anyone admitted with a temporary visa who later wants to remain in the United States on a permanent basis would have to become a US citizen to remain. We should make it a severe crime for anyone to knowingly employ or hire illegal immigrants. And illegal immigrants, since they should not be here, should be prohibited from owning property, driving, or receiving government entitlements. There is no reason why we can't continue to be a country with a melting pot of cultures and beliefs—but one with realistic population growth controls. Immigration is to be added to the platform issues."

Hugo poured himself another cup of coffee. Then continued. "We've listed some real problems to address. But let's not overlook the sad shape of the legislative branch. It needs a cultural change. Members of Congress tend to vote as a partisan block, rather than each legislator voting on the basis of what he or she feels is best for our country. Does every Republican legislator feel pressure from the Republican Party to vote the same way on abortion and the right to live issues? Does every Democratic Party legislator feel pressure from the Democratic Party to vote the same way on, say, gun control legislation? Is there so much polarization in Congress today that Republican legislators would never cross the aisle to vote favorably on a bill sponsored by a Democrat? And vice versa. We discussed this at length at lunch Friday." Hugo thought any change in the legislative process should begin with breaking down the partisan barrier between members of Congress so that a legislator would not feel compelled to vote on legislative matters the way his or her party wants the legislator to vote—rather than voting for what's in the best interest of the country. "I'm not sure how I would break down the barrier, but I want to make **Party Line Voting** a platform issue. I would open the door to any realistic approach to improving an existing crippled legislative process."

Hugo was reluctant to express as part of his platform his personal thoughts on the other candidates. He could have told Macey that under our system of electing a president, the presidential choices are limited to politicians who already have been tainted by partisan politics. But he didn't. Or he could have said that none of the other candidates speak out on important matters affecting our country. But he didn't. And he could have said both the probable major party nominees are too old, not qualified to lead, not respected as global leaders, border on senility, or have personal agendas not favorable to voters. But he didn't.

"The **space program** is another issue I want as part of my platform," said Hugo. "Why? Because no other presidential candidate has discussed the importance of exploring or controlling the vast space above Earth and beyond. It's important. Ask Elon Musk." Hugo wanted the public to be aware that whichever country controls space will control life on Earth. "Do you think all those *weather satellites* that have rocketed up for the past sixty-five years are all weather related? I don't think so! The safety and security of the United States will depend in large part on who controls outer space. Unfortunately, voters aren't tuned in to the importance of our space program. But they should be! No country should exclusively control outer space activities. I'm not aware of any presidential candidates including Biden or Trump, talking about the control of outer space."

"Mace, I want to limit my campaign platform to those six major issues. I know there are many more concerns which could be addressed, such as health care, global warming, energy, and water shortage. I'll address those concerns when asked. What do you think, Mace? Can you and your Group put together campaign information with what I have furnished?"

Macey had a legal pad full of comments. He had more than enough information to put together a formal campaign platform, hardcopy campaign literature, and marketing material for internet distribution. He was ready to roll and bubbling with enthusiasm. Macey told Hugo he would be flying back to Durham on Tuesday to meet with his team. "Give me a couple of days, Mr. McCormick. You won't be disappointed."

"Louise and I have made the commitment, Mace. We're in it to the end. Just keep hammering home my slogan: 'No More Small Talk.'"

GOOD LUCK, HUGO

CHAPTER 27

The Hartford Globe Offices
11/13/2023

★ ★ ★

At 6:45 am Jack Lambert pulled his 2023 charcoal black BMW sports sedan into his parking space beneath the ground floor of the office building he owned in Hartford. He couldn't help but notice that Hugo's car already was in the space reserved for him.

"Hugo! What the hell are you doing here? I thought you had another job," said Jack rhetorically.

Hugo arrived at his office early to write what he had expected would be his last editorial for at least nine years. Jack, who already gave his blessings to Hugo to pursue a new job, told Hugo he would give him a nine-month consulting salary and thereafter an indefinite unpaid leave of absence.

Nevertheless, Hugo felt obligated to write one more column, the purpose being to explain to his followers the reason why they would no longer be seeing his editorials in the newspapers. This last editorial would give him the opportunity to jumpstart his campaign to become the president.

Hugo's writing style was consistent regardless of subject matter: simple, concise, to the point, and easy to understand. His editorial would be appearing in the editorial section of next Sunday's

Hartford Globe and in other national newspapers which purchased his syndicated columns.

No More Small Talk

by

Hugo McCormick, Candidate for President of the United States

Former Congressman from Connecticut and now syndicated editorialist with *The Hartford Globe*.

"It's almost election time, time for us to begin thinking about who should be the next president of the United States. For the past seventeen years I have been writing, lecturing, and giving speeches on topics often ignored by politicians, but which need dialogue and leadership. I was overwhelmed by the enthusiastic support for my views by my followers' via e-mails, letters, and telephone calls.

"I hesitate to find fault with any of the candidates now running for the presidency. They're all hard working, civic minded citizens, I'm sure ... intelligent and willing to serve in the most responsible and prestigious job in the world. I could but won't question the integrity of any of them. I accept all of the candidates for what they probably are, well-intended persons.

"Having said that, Joe Biden and Donald Trump, the probable presidential nominees of the two major political parties, both are products of political machines which every four years control the names of the persons who will be on the presidential ballot on Election Day. Democrats and Republicans alike typically select from within their ranks nominees who have paid their dues as politicians, have political support from colleagues, and are electable. Nominees typically believe voters, when deciding for whom to vote, will cast their votes based on party affiliation, personality differences, charm, race, sex, religion, or other factors—placing little importance on the views and leadership qualifications of the nominee. Negative campaigning through tearing down the character and capability of a nominee's opponent has become the strategy of nominees.

"Which of the probable nominees has discussed what they would do to encourage peace between the Israelis and Palestinians? I don't mean a mere cease fire as that's not a solution for peace. The continuing dispute between these two countries has caused tensions among many other countries supporting either Israel or Palestine. It's time for a permanent solution between the two countries.

"Which of the probable nominees has discussed an acceptable solution to the Russia-Ukraine conflict? What is an acceptable solution?

'Which of the probable nominees has the political guts to talk about the great disparity in incomes between the grossly overpaid and the underpaid? Who has the political courage to encourage legislation which will put more money in the pockets of the lower income earners to allow then to share in the American Dream? Which of the nominees has the political guts to discuss imposing a high tax rate of 80 to 85 per cent on net annual incomes exceeding, say, fifty million dollars?

"Which of the probable nominees has offered solutions to the substantial rise in gangs, crimes, and the trafficking of illegal drugs?

"What are the probable nominees saying about our energy policies other than the need for a change? We know the problem. We need a solution.

"And what do our probable nominees think about the control of outer space? Yes, we have a space program, but shouldn't we give it more importance? Why don't the probable nominees talk about what would happen if another country, like China or Russia, assumed exclusive control of outer space? Would we then find ourselves hostages to a country which for years has sought our demise?

"There are many other important concerns which are not being addressed by the probable nominees. Why not? May I suggest that to do so might require expressing an opinion and a nominee could wave goodbye to any voter who disagreed with the nominee's opinion.

"Look at the 2024 probable presidential nominees for the next election. They're all intelligent, granted. But they seem to think that the best path to becoming elected is to emphasize party affiliation and to outbash their opponent. How many voters will go to the polls on Election Day voting against a candidate rather than for a candidate?'

"I'm not happy with the presidential choices destined to appear on the 2024 election ballot. So, I've decided to challenge the two probable major party nominees, Joe Biden and Donald Trump. This will be my last editorial for a while—hopefully for a period equal to the next two terms of the presidency. I have been encouraged to run for the presidency by a group of young but bright college students who share the belief that it's time for a change in the way a president is elected. They will be my start-up team, and you will be hearing from us shortly.

"*No More Small Talk* will be my campaign slogan. If elected, I intend to provide the leadership to consider and advance solutions to the problems we face today, including changing the existing political process to allow voters better choices for those seeking to become president. I am counting on the people who agree with me to support my effort."

CHAPTER 28

Campaign Progress, The Birth of PPP
12/2023

★ ★ ★

Hugo's grass roots campaign was progressing better than expected. Just shy of one month since he announced he'd run and the party already had raised forty-five million dollars, primarily from contributions ranging from ten to one hundred dollars. A few corporate donors gave considerably more. Hugo made it clear to the Group of Five that he would accept donations from all donors ... with the proviso that he wanted no donations from persons or entities with either criminal ties or who expected political favors. "My position on the platform issues will make it clear: I will not exchange my political beliefs for campaign funds."

Hugo's team, which originally consisted of the Group of Five, now had increased to over 500. Liz and Blair were instrumental in establishing a network of volunteers in every state and in Puerto Rico. Each state was divided into three or more sections, each section with volunteer captains heading up funding efforts. Each captain was screened for honesty, loyalty, leadership, and most importantly, motivation to support Hugo and his campaign to the end.

Justin's role as a member of the team was to set up the political structure and mechanics required for Hugo's name to be on the state ballots. He didn't have a clue where to start, but he did know that a good beginning was to contact Seymour Weinstein, a second-year law student at Duke.

Seymour, who liked to be called Si, volunteered to help with the campaign in response to a solicitation for volunteers Macey had posted in the building housing Duke's Law School. Si saw his involvement as a chance to get his feet wet in a career he hoped to pursue after graduation. Si's grandfather had been a lawyer and congressman, and his father practiced law for 21 years before being appointed a federal judge. Si liked what they did for a living, including their lifestyles. As a law school freshman, Si had taken classes in Constitutional Law and Corporate Law. "I don't know Hugo," said Si. "But I like what he says, and I certainly won't be voting for either Biden or Trump. I want to help."

Justin already had preliminary negotiations with Practical Party of the People, a registered political organization that now was dormant. After discussions with Hugo and Macey, Justin was authorized to consummate the acquisition of the rights to the organization on terms already agreed. Si agreed to assist in formalizing the acquisition of the inactive registered entity.

"The first step in organizing a new political party in the United States is to think of a name, hold a meeting, and then appoint temporary officials to office," said Si. "Nothing special about the organizational meeting. It can be in the parking lot for all it really matters. At a minimum, leadership initially should include a Committee Chairman and a Treasurer."

Hugo, Macey and Justin previously had already given the party name some thought. They didn't want the party name to infer anything characteristic of what other party names stood for. They certainly didn't want to be identified with the stereotyped beliefs and values of the Democratic and Republican parties ... or the Green Party ...

or any party name which gave the perception of having socialism or communism philosophies or connections. The three agreed to retain the name Practical Party of the People ... or, for short, PPP.

Si agreed to do what was required legally to formally re-establish PPP as a political entity. "We'll need to file financial documents and disclosures with the Federal Election Commission once contributions or expenditures become meaningful. I'll request governmental advisory opinions approving our status as a legitimate party. The Federal Election Commission will want to see if our party has nominated a qualified candidate for President, and that we commence engaging in certain activities evidencing party intent ... such as voter registration, party support drives, publicly publishing a party platform, holding a national convention, setting up a national office, and establishing state affiliates." Si said these are mere formalities which should consist of not much more than time, thought, and paperwork.

Justin advised Si that Macey presently is running the show as the Chairman, and that the party is well under way with fund raising. "We already have established PPP bank accounts in every state with a master clearing account at Bank of America in Durham. Contributions are pouring into the bank accounts ... and are being transferred to the clearing account daily. Our national office has rented space in downtown Durham ... and we have affiliate locations in every state. If you need the particulars, I will get them," said Justin.

"Sounds like you guys have been busy," said Si. "Once PPP formally is up and running, you will need to elect permanent leadership and adopt a Charter and Bylaws. In essence, the Charter and Bylaws will be the constitution of the party. It will outline the party organization, the relationships between other party organizations, the basis on which the party is founded and the goals and intents of the party. A few caveats," said Si. "Keep meticulous notes. Every dollar raised and spent must be accounted for and reported to the FEC as well as to committee members, party leadership, and the public. You should record minutes of every meeting, the decisions voted for and against, officers elected, fundraising, voters registered in the party, voter registration drives, and whatever else is significant. Just expect that someone, particularly your opposition, at some point will scrutinize every move the party makes."

CHAPTER 29

Port Royal Plantation, Hilton Head Island
12/9/2023

Hugo was pooped—very pooped. On Sunday morning, December 3rd, he was in Washington, DC for a scheduled 15 minute taped interview with a Fox TV news anchor—the interview to be aired later that day on the six o'clock Fox News channel. Late Sunday afternoon he met with staffers in New York City to discuss plans for a speech in Madison Square Garden on June 30th.

On Monday, he spent most of the morning at his home in Connecticut discussing campaign strategy by telephone with Macey and Blair. Then in the afternoon, he made plans with staffers for campaign stops the following morning in Boston, Massachusetts and Stamford, Connecticut, finishing the day with a fund-raising dinner in Greenwich, Connecticut.

On Wednesday, the 6th of December, he spent the morning prepping for an 8 pm online town hall meeting that night in Philadelphia. Then on the 7th of December, he had breakfast with staffers in Philadelphia, made three short five-minute videos to be seen later on national television channels, including CNN, NBC, ABC and Fox News. Later that evening, he was the key speaker at a coat and tie dinner affair at the Sheraton Hotel on Market Street in Philadelphia. He gave a speech to a group of young business leaders on the importance of presidential image in global affairs.

Early the next morning he was in Roanoke, Virginia for an 8 o'clock breakfast meeting with the Governor of Virginia, Glen Younglin, to discuss the need for someone to challenge Biden and Trump in the presidential election. Later on the 8th of December, Hugo drove to the Marriott Hotel in Columbia, South Carolina, where breakfast was scheduled the following morning in the ballroom with an audience of one hundred forty-five South Carolinians who wanted to personally meet Hugo.

So, Hugo was very tired when he and two of his staffers arrived around 1:40 pm on December 9th at the security gate in Port Royal Plantation. The Plantation, a rather upscale private residential community on the Port Royal Sound side of Hilton Head Island, was located off U.S. 278—in the middle of the Island. Homes within the Plantation ranged in value between $900M to $20MM. Residents on the Island typically were a mixed voting class. This year had been shaping up to be another election year where the voters had limited choices in terms of the presidential nominees and would most likely cast their votes along party lines—or for the least disliked nominee. Hugo was scheduled to give an informal speech to Port Royal Plantation residents at Port Royal Plantation's Beach Club.

Hugo was greeted at the Plantation business office by Terp Davis, long time manager of Port Royal Plantation. Terp didn't arrange the get-to-know the candidate gathering. He was either smart enough to be aloof from politics or just plain lazy. Rather, the gathering was arranged by a group of politically savvy, but angered residents, who were finding it difficult to vote for either Biden or Trump. Terp had agreed to escort Hugo to the Club to meet with residents at 2 p.m. Since Hugo was a bit early, Terp gave Hugo and his staffers a brief tour of the plantation, stopping first at historic Fort Walker, then past the infamous 1900 circa steam cannon, then past an architectural civil war reconstructed replica of the Pope House, and then down North Port Royal Drive to the Beach Club.

Cocktails and light snacks were made available to the attendees—and to Hugo. Hugo limited himself to one vodka martini. After Terp said a few words of introduction, Hugo gave a short speech highlighting the six key issues in his platform, and the things he proposed to do if elected. He was asked many questions relating to illegal immigration, his thoughts on how to resolve the turmoil in the Mideast, his attitude toward China and other powerful global leaders, entitlement programs, and the limited choices voters have in presidential elections. After an hour of responding to questions, Hugo said that unlike his presidential opponents, his views and thoughts on matters which should concern voters are candid and transparent—and can be examined in detail in the book he recently published: *No More Small Talk.*

Contemplating a few of the attendees might accuse Hugo of coming to Hilton Head Island for the purpose of "hawking" his book, Hugo said, "I wrote *No More Small Talk* because I had strong feelings about critical issues that affect all of us Americans, issues which are not being discussed or even identified by our present leaders or the other presidential nominees. Even if you don't vote for me, you owe it to yourselves to demand the other nominees tell you what they plan to do about the important issues which concern our country. Don't let them stonewall you. You deserve answers.

"My staff has brought copies of my book for those who are interested. The book will cost you $28. I don't want anything from the sale. So, I'll give you a copy—but only if you make a $28 contribution to either Habitat for Humanity or to The Hilton Head Foundation."

Without consulting Terp, Hugo said, "Unless he objects, and I hope he won't, I'll leave the books in the good hands of Terp Davis, hoping he and the Plantation staff will coordinate payment of any funds received from the sale of the books to the two causes."

Hugo sat down to an enthusiastic standing ovation. A group of some 50 persons huddled around Terp ready to purchase copies of his book. Another group had gathered outside the Beach Club waiting to express thanks to Hugo for bringing common sense to the Plantation and putting a little spirit into the presidential election.

Hugo spent the remainder of the day on the Island at the Westin Hotel. Tomorrow his schedule said he would be driving to the Hilton Head-Savannah Airport and boarding a flight to Atlanta, Georgia.

CHAPTER 30

Atlanta, Georgia
12/10/2023

With a name like McCormick, there was no question about whether Hugo was an Irishman. He was as Irish as an Irishman could be. He was a third generation Irishman, so he didn't have a brogue—like many of his third generation Irish friends did. Atlanta has an Irish population that ranks seventh among cities in the United States.

Hugo had been invited to a brunch in the Buckhead section of Atlanta five months ago to celebrate the opening of a new Irish pub near the Buckhead Mall. The pub was appropriately named Brian's Irish Eatery. Brian and Hugo were classmates in high school, and they maintained a close friendship ever since. Hugo accepted the invitation long before he had any thoughts of being a presidential candidate.

Hugo had planned to mingle with the crowd, and then give a speech about the long historical involvement of the Irish community in Atlanta. But he changed the script somewhat once he entered the presidential race. Aware that he now would be receiving national coverage, he saw an opportunity to discuss his thoughts on the income insufficiency of many hard-working, low-income earners in the United States, and a proposal he had to change the tax laws to put more money into their pockets.

When local Irish leaders in the Atlanta area heard Hugo would be in town on December 10th, invitations were sent to him inviting him to be a guest at a few other functions. He had been invited to activities at the Get Lucky Festival at Park Tavern, the Smyrna Market Village Christmas Festival, and holiday festivities at both Murphy's Bar and Pub 71. But his presence at Brian's brunch in Buckhead and a few words to the patrons were enough for him.

The brunch was held under an enormous carnival type tent adjacent to the pub. It started at 11 am. The menu featured Derby sage cheese, braised short ribs, Yukon gold garlic mashed potatoes, steamed potatoes, home-style baked beans, brown bread, and green salad. Water and soft drinks were served. However most of the guests preferred the other drinks being served—Vino Verde from Portugal and green beer from a barrel, reportedly imported from Ireland.

Hugo's name and reputation had been plastered all over town to drum up a big attendance for the brunch. Not surprisingly the Irish turned out in droves—not necessarily to hear Hugo speak as much as to get an early start on what appeared to be the makings of a fine old Irish celebration. Three hundred fifty tickets were sold for the brunch.

After the main course, Hugo was called to the podium to say a few words. The Chairperson for the event, Michael Cronin, who showed some signs of already having tested more green beer than he should have, introduced Hugo as the next president of the United States and the most prestigious Irishman to participate in Irish festivities in Atlanta since John Kennedy in the early 1960s.

Hugo rose to a rowdy, but enthusiastic applause. He understood that this was a day of celebration for the Irish and the new Irish pub, and he didn't want to smother the patrons with political talk. He was also aware that several local reporters would be on hand to search for a political message in whatever he had to say. "Thanks for the flattering remarks, Mike. And thank you all for attending. First, I want to set the record straight. Contrary to what you might be thinking, I recognize there are far more important things to do today than listening to political blarney from a fellow Irishman—so my words will be very brief. I understand what the priorities are today. Second, if I am the most prestigious Irishman to visit Atlanta since JFK, then I would have to accuse your Chairperson, Mike Cronin, of already feeding us all a bit of blarney.

"But on a serious note, I do want to say a couple things that I know are meaningful to me—and should be meaningful to you. I want to talk about something the other presidential nominees, Biden and Trump, have talked about obliquely, but so far have not offered solutions that are simple, understandable, or that might work. And that is how to put more money in the pockets of those who have yet to share in the American Dream."

Hugo spoke generally for fifteen minutes about his proposal to change the tax laws so that persons or families receiving net incomes of less than one hundred fifty thousand dollars would pay no federal income taxes, thus giving them more spending options. Hugo didn't go into much detail about his proposal because he sensed that most of the audience, though they might have liked his proposal, preferred to do what they came for—drink at least a few mugs of Irish beer.

So, he wrapped up his speech and walked away from the podium hearing the kind of appreciative applause one usually receives when cutting short what could have been a lengthy speech.

CHAPTER 31

Ten-Day Campaign Trip to the Midwest
12/2023

★ ★ ★

In Midwestern cities and towns, the concept of illegal immigration was easily understood by the working man—more illegal immigrants equated to fewer jobs for American citizens—pure and simple. Typical Midwesterners had an immediate solution to the problem. If persons illegally entered the United States, for whatever reason, once detected, there should be a quick exit out. Any immigrant who stayed beyond the expiration of their visa, should be shown the same route.

On December 13th Hugo left his home in Connecticut and he and his wife flew to Chicago to bring his campaign to the Midwestern states. Hugo, his wife, and local staffers toured the major hub cities from Chicago to Detroit, Columbus, St. Louis, Indianapolis, Milwaukee, Cleveland, Kansas City and then back to Chicago. Liz, who coordinated Hugo's visits with the local volunteer staff, accompanied Hugo on the tour.

Hugo's primary mission was to talk about platform issues, but he knew he had to emphasize one important issue that directly affected Midwesterners' pocketbooks—immigration. So, his plans for handling the immigration issues were discussed at length at each stop.

Hugo didn't sugarcoat his message. "I'm for enforcing vehemently our existing policy of not allowing illegal immigrants to enter or remain in our country. I'm also in favor of a policy which limits the number of immigrants annually permitted entrance into our country, and for investigating the backgrounds of all those who enter the United States on a permanent or temporary basis—whether work-related or as visitors.

"I see our policy as being twofold: We must deal with those who now live in our country as illegal immigrants, and we must have a clear definitive policy regarding future immigrants entering our country."

Hugo didn't limit his remarks to immigration. He spoke about the substantial increase in crimes in the major cities, many crimes attributable to drugs and drug trafficking—and what he would do if elected president. He talked about income disparity and the need to find a way to put more money into the pockets of the *have nots*. And he didn't shy away from responding to any concerns raised by those who attended his speaking events.

Everywhere Hugo went during his Midwest tour he was greeted by enthusiastic crowds. Hugo was not one for small talk, wide smiles, giving autographs, kissing babies, or acting pompously. Though not one terribly impressed by large crowds, even he was overwhelmed by the chants of "No More Small Talk" by enthusiastic crowds as he traveled from one stop to another. Hugo was not only flattered, but at O'Hara International Airport, on his return flight to Durham, he sensed for the first time that he just might have a good shot at winning the presidency.

Hugo's next stop was to PPP's headquarters in Durham, North Carolina, a city he once called home.

CHAPTER 32

National Office of PPP
Downtown Durham, NC
12/22/2023

★ ★ ★

Locals were surprisingly pleased that downtown Durham now was the site of a national office of a political party important enough to have a candidate running for the presidency of the United States.

Durham is located 23 miles from the Virginia border, 140 miles from the Appalachian highlands, 130 miles from the Atlantic Coast, midway between Miami and Chicago and midway between Atlanta and Philadelphia. It was known as both a textile and tobacco town back in the 1800s and remained so until the 1950s and 1960s.

If you worked or lived within 10 miles of the Chesterfield manufacturing facilities on North Main Street, you didn't have to be a smoker to inhale and taste unfiltered nicotine that roamed like heavy mist throughout the city and beyond. Years ago, the locals considered nicotine mist to be one of the fringe benefits of living near the manufacturing facilities. Today, many class action law firms throughout the country have made fortunes bringing class action lawsuits against tobacco companies for alleged deaths and life threatening cancers resulting from the use or exposure to the ingredients lingering in the nicotine mist.

Durham has changed since the early days. It now is a city with a population of approximately 220,000, and its population has become more diverse with the added corporate presence of Research Triangle Park, GE Aircraft Engines, Freudenberg Nonwovens, and AW North Carolina.

Durham was chosen as the national office of PPP because Hugo was a graduate of Duke, the founders of the revamped PPP party were Duke Students, and its corporate legal adviser, albeit on a pro bono basis, was a second-year student at the Duke Law School.

Macey had negotiated a two-year lease for a small two-story office building on Main Street near the Marriott Hotel. The building was not fancy, but the price was right. Nothing structurally had to be done to the interior to make the building suitable for its short-term needs.

The second floor had a large corner office, which Macey reserved for Hugo, and seven smaller offices, one occupied by Macey and another occupied by Blair. The other offices were not assigned but could be used by any of the staff when privacy was needed. Liz, Crystal, and Justin had desk space in an open area on the first floor where they would be the first to be seen by anyone who entered the building. The first floor also had a 18 x 20 foot conference room with a large oblong well-used tan mahogany conference table, twelve dark blue fabric backed metal chairs, a pull down projector screen, a 4 x 8 foot presentation board, and a large picture of downtown Durham hanging on the wall.

Macey had scheduled a team meeting for seven o'clock in the evening. The team had grown from five to seventeen, twelve being added within the past month to assume responsibilities within an organization experiencing a need for more managers.

Hugo would be making his initial campaign visit to Durham the next day, so Macey wanted to greet him with a well-informed staff, an organization equipped to efficiently run a successful campaign, and facilities adequate to evidence that PPP was *in it for the long run.*

Additionally, Macey wanted to reacquaint Hugo to the first paid member of the organizational team, Joe Buck, a well-known political marketing strategist with a reputation among the media for being honest and trustworthy. Donor contributions were much more than anticipated, making it possible to retain Joe Buck and a few other professionals with campaign skills and experience—professionals with the political savvy to communicate Hugo's platform to the most persons in the shortest period.

The conference table allowed twelve people to sit comfortably. The conference room was small, but adequate. Eleven team members were present as Macey opened the meeting. "Before we start, to those who have not already met him, let me introduce Joe Buck. Joe joined us a few days ago to help with the scheduling of online town hall meetings and other appearances for Hugo. Most of you have heard or read about Joe—so I won't dwell on his credentials. He's a professional. He gets things done. And, most importantly, we need him now. Joe has a lot of good thoughts about communicating Hugo's message to voters—Joe."

Joe Buck stood up and said he was happy to be part of Hugo's team. "I've known Hugo personally for at least fifteen years—and you've backing a winner. I like what he says, but more importantly so do many others. Mace has asked me to put together a schedule of personal appearances and town hall meetings, so I'll need your input. Hugo is only one person. His presence can't be spread too thin. We want to use his communicative skills effectively."

"Tomorrow morning Hugo's paying us a visit," said Macey.

"He'll be arriving at Raleigh-Durham Airport around ten and staying at the downtown Marriott." Macey then proceeded around the table for input by the committee. Notes of the meeting were being taken by Sybil Kotar, one of three full-time paid assistants hired by Macey to keep the paperwork and schedules organized.

Justin informed the committee that all the corporate paperwork has been filed and approved. ''PPP now is a legitimate national political party. You're sitting in our national office," said Justin. "And thanks to Si Weinstein, we now have affiliated campaign offices in each state. Si has been a workhorse. He has been handling all our organizational paperwork—for free. He has gone well beyond the limits of what we requested of him. Si recommends that we now retain an outside law firm as PPP needs specialized legal representation. I agree."

"We have enough money in the coffers now," said Blair. Blair, who volunteered to serve as Treasurer, assumed the responsibilities of raising campaign funds and accounting for all monies received. "As of December 15th, we have raised slightly more than $45,000,000—and the money keeps rolling in. Our expenses so far are approximately $15,250,000."

Blair stated Si had helped him establish bank accounts in all the states and that all accounts are in compliance with the federal campaign funding laws. "We now need a CPA firm to handle reporting and financial accounting. Though we're a tax-exempt organization, there's still lots of paperwork to be filed. I agree with Justin that we're getting too big to be without lawyers and accountants to help us. I suggest a law firm and CPA firm be hired immediately to keep us out of jail."

There was little discussion. Everyone knew it was the thing to do. Macey agreed to handle the hiring of a law firm, while Blair said he's already talked to two CPA firms with offices in Durham. To cover all bases and at the suggestion of Si, the Committee passed a resolution formally naming Hugo as PPP's nominee for the presidency.

Blair then commented that Liz and Crystal should be applauded for their work in expanding the volunteer organizational structure from a handful of persons to some 75 to 100 volunteers in each state. "We're talking about 4,000 volunteers. I'll let Liz and Crystal report on the status of the volunteers. I also would like to point out that the donations we received so far in December far exceeded the December contributions reported by the other major parties combined—a message which tells me that we are on a fast track. We keep ten to twenty thousand dollars in the operating accounts in each of the states. The rest is funneled into a master clearing account here in Durham. We have about $30,000,000 deposited in a Money Manager Account with Bank of America. We receive interest in the four per cent range."

Crystal and Liz then gave an update on how they had structured the volunteer program. Liz reported she had been traveling and interviewing the people selected to be volunteer captains in the respective states. "Each state has a volunteer captain, a volunteer staff of at least 75 persons, and a bank account with operating funds of no more than $20,000 at any one time. Blair's signature is required on all expense checks exceeding $5,000. Each captain was authorized to hire a full-time secretary and, if needed, a part-time secretary. Volunteers were encouraged to contact persons throughout their respective voting areas, disseminating information about Hugo through eyeball contact, internet messages and hard copy pamphlets. Equally as important, volunteers were asked to follow up with donors to encourage them to request their friends and acquaintances to also support Hugo by becoming donors."

Crystal said she was constantly updating an organizational chart which linked the names, faces, and backgrounds of the volunteers throughout the organization. "It's overwhelming," said Crystal. "I can't keep up with all the volunteers. If all the people who expressed an interest in becoming a volunteer voted, Hugo would be a shoe-in. We tell anyone who has expressed an interest in being a volunteer that they have been placed on a volunteer list—to be contacted if the need arises. We don't want to turn off any person interested in volunteering."

Liz continued by saying she and Crystal prepared a form letter which was mailed to blocks of persons identified from mailing lists procured from marketing sources. The letter was e-mail formatted with the intent of being sent by volunteers to friends, acquaintances, and anyone else who had identifiable e-mail addresses. The letter identified who Hugo was, why he was seeking election to the presidency, his political platform, and the reasons why the recipients should vote for him. Donations were requested from those sent letters. Hugo approved and signed the letter. Liz passed out a copy of the letter to those in the room. The form letter stated:

> Greetings: Not long ago, I was asked if I would be interested in running for the position of president of the United States. I was humbled to be asked. After considerable thought, I said yes. So now I am a candidate.
>
> Why am I a candidate? Well, as you know, your options for electing a president now appear to be limited to one of two persons, Joe Biden or Donald Trump. This doesn't give voters much of a choice. We had the same limited choice in the last presidential election in 2020. Biden won, but Trump and his MAGA followers insists the election was "rigged," and he should be president. For the past three years, Biden and Trump have been at each other's throat over age, character, and personality issues. Trump is a defendant in three significant federal criminal lawsuits and one state civil lawsuit, all being hotly contested. Trump has let it be known that if he is elected president, he will consider bringing retribution legal charges against many who opposed his views during the past few years. Do you know why you'll vote for either come election day? I don't! That's why I accepted the request that I run for the presidency.
>
> How should we measure the qualifications and capabilities of the candidates running for the presidency?

First, let's examine leadership of the nominees. This is important. It is critical that the next president not only be a leader, but a leader respected within the United States and by the leaders of other countries. We should examine the leadership qualifications and capabilities of the nominees.

Hard to measure, isn't it? Neither Biden nor Trump are popular among members of their own parties, neither are liked by most voters beyond their hard-core voter base, leaders of foreign countries do not look favorable upon either Biden or Trump as an effective global leader, and they're both contentious super seniors who might lack the stamina to effectively manage our country for the next four years. In my case, I don't have much of a political resume with which you can assess my leadership qualities. But do I need to have a long political rap sheet to evidence my leadership qualifications? I have a record in the private sector which speaks for itself. Now you must make a choice as to who among the nominees will be the most effective leader.

Next you should examine the personal character and qualifications of each of the candidates—like intelligence, vision, honesty, trustworthiness, and decision-making capability, all important criteria for the next president. Again, hard to measure. But you must weigh these matters when you decide for whom to vote.

Equally as important as the above are the views of the candidates on issues of importance, and how each will manage the important issues if elected. I've listed below what I consider the important concerns which the next president should address:

- Seeking and pursuing a path which ultimately will lead to world peace among all nations.

- Narrowing the income gap between the haves and the have-nots without jeopardizing the fundamentals of the free enterprise system upon which our society is premised.

- Recognizing the problems underlying violent crimes, gangs and drugs, and effectively implementing social, economic and legal reforms to eradicate or minimize these activities.

- Recognizing the need for us to work with other major countries to manage and control outer space so that one country will never have exclusive control over outer space activities.

- Implementing a meaningful and effective immigration policy which will prohibit illegal immigrants from entering our country.

- Working with legislators of all political parties to eliminate the present partisan culture among legislators so that our now crippled Congress can legislate more efficiently and effectively.

Where do the other candidates stand on these issues? I don't know. I suggest voters should ask them.

Where do I stand on these issues? You can visit my website at *www.nomoresmalltalk.org* where I disclose my thoughts in detail. Or you can research the archives of *The Hartford Globe* to view my commentary on many of these same areas of concern. Or you might consider reading my recent book: *No More Small Talk*.

So, I'm running for the presidency of the United States because I feel the issues that are important to you and me are not being adequately addressed by the existing candidates. I have offered solutions. And I pledge that whatever action I take as your president will be in the best interests of 'we the people', and not in the best interest of me or the party that elected me as it's nominee.

This election is about important things. The Democrats and Republicans have demonstrated their ability to raise an astonishing amount of money for their campaigns. Soon I suspect a meaningful portion of these resources will be focused on negative campaigning against me. I'd rather have my opponents spend their campaign money explaining to voters what they think and what to expect of them if elected president. They haven't so far, and I doubt that they will.

I'm sending this message to you for two reasons: (1) I would like your vote if you agree that I would be a better president than

Biden or Trump; and (2) I would appreciate your financial support for my campaign in any amount you may choose to make.

Thank you,

Hugo McCormick, PPP Candidate for President of the United States

Breakfast with Joe Buck
12/23/2023

★ ★ ★

Fire and Brimstone was not Hugo's style. But Joe thought occasionally it should be. The two sat alone having breakfast at the Marriott coffee shop. It was early—about 6:30 a.m.

"The other candidates are vulnerable," said Joe. "Hit 'em where it hurts. The Democrats are split over who should be the presidential nominee, Joe Biden or anybody else. He's now 81 and showing signs of creeping senility. Many Democrats believe the future of the Democratic Party would be better served with a younger, more spirited nominee. But Joe Biden is the incumbent, and that carries lots of weight with party-line voters.

"The Republican Party also is in trouble. Many Republicans have differing views as to who should be that party's nominee. Other than his often rowdy cult followers, support for Trump among many party loyalists is lukewarm. Many Republican incumbants are afraid to oppose him for fear of his retaliatory tactics, but insiders might like to see him step aside. However, Trump is far ahead in the polls of any the other Republican candidates seeking election, and most think he'll be the Party's nominee. The prize is yours for the taking. You can't win if you don't fight for it, Hugo." Joe leaned back in his chair and raised a taunting finger at Hugo— "It's time to kick ass."

Hugo had known Joe for years. Not intimately, but well enough to know that they didn't see eye to eye on many things. Joe was well respected in campaign circles. He usually produced winners. But there was something about Joe of which Hugo was not particularly fond—his reputed style of *taking no prisoners*. Nevertheless, Hugo's campaign needed a few more voices with experience, and he gave way to Macey's suggestion that Joe be hired.

"Hugo, I got a busy schedule for you this week. Two charitable events, a luncheon speech, and a press conference. And on January 7th, you've been asked to appear on Face the Press—for an hour! You've got to go on the attack. Your opponents are vulnerable. You got an old man, an obnoxious bully, and a few *wantabees*."

"Attack what?" said Hugo. "I'm not going to engage in mudslinging. I don't have to! Mudslinging does little to define who I am. What defines me is best described in what I've written about for years. Why do you think my editorials were labeled *No More Small Talk*? Because there's too much bull shit in politics and elections, too much irrelevancy, too much bickering and bantering, and too much negative campaigning."

Hugo paused for a moment. He was heated. And he noticed shades of embarrassment surfacing in Joe's face. "Joe, I'm running because I don't think Biden or Trump see a need to convince voters why they deserve to be elected. They think the election is between the two of them, so they'll continue to tear each other apart to see who comes out on top. And while I'm at it, I don't make personal appearances at charitable events just to get votes. I feel it's demeaning to produce a fake smile, shake hands with persons you don't know and will never see again, or kiss babies. That may be the style of others, but not for me."

Hugo and Joe went back and forth on how each thought the campaign should be conducted. Joe, a savvy political strategist, realized he couldn't convince Hugo otherwise, so he softened his strategic approach to yield to the desires of his candidate.

Hugo, on the other hand, was a political realist. He knew he might have to shade his political convictions a bit ... or he might not have another opportunity to advance his political views. So, like most politicians, the two compromised. Hugo was not going to attend charitable events merely because others thought it was the thing to do to attract votes, but he did say he would make himself available to a press that would insist that he comment on the qualifications and views of his opponents. Hugo agreed to make an appearance on Face the Press on January 7th.

Alistair

CHAPTER 34

Face the Press
1/7/2024

Though President Biden might serve as the whipping boy for many politicians and political pundits, he created this environment himself, because he is less accessible to the press than the candidates seeking to replace him. During the past six months, there were four controlled Republican Party debates featuring Republican candidates.

During the debates, responses to questions too often had little bearing to the questions asked—spin and bashing each other were at its best. Donald Trump saw no benefit to participating in these so-called debates. He was so far ahead in the polls that he could sit back and let the other candidates do harm to each other, or so he thought. In fact, the polling numbers for Trump increased after each debate, notwithstanding his lack of presence on the stage.

Understandably, both leading candidates for the major party nominee slots, Biden and Trump, were reluctant to engage in formal *give and take* with reporters. To do so might expose them into giving opinions on sensitive issues they would prefer to avoid—or they knew little about. As Hugo said in a recent editorial relating to campaigning, "Politicians don't volunteer thoughts on critical national issues, unless painted into a corner. Rather, they would prefer to sniff out hot button issues in a particular region of the country, then craft positions popular to the voters in that area."

Face the Press is an hour-long Sunday midmorning TV program patterned along the lines of *Meet the Press*. The program features one-on-one interviews by the host with guests then in the news. The host, now in his 12th year as the moderator, is Alistair MacDougal, former editor of *Washington Today* and a Pulitzer Prize winner in 2007 for distinguished editorial commentary. Alistair had a reputation for asking tough, penetrating questions, the type most guests would rather sidestep. And through persistency, he would push and push and push his guests until he heard a response close to what he was seeking.

Members of President Biden's cabinet and members of Congress were frequent guests. So were controversial foreign dignitaries, including diplomats from the Middle Eastern countries. President Biden and Donald Trump were invited to appear on several occasions, but declined. Hugo needed to play catch-up in the campaign, so he accepted the invitation to appear at 11 a.m. on January 7, 2024—with a *no heads-up briefing* of what topics would be discussed.

"Good morning and welcome again to *Face the Press*. My name is Alistair MacDougal. I am your host. As you know, we are amid what appears to be an exciting presidential election. The Democrats will nominate Joe Biden, who will be seeking a second term. And the Republicans will nominate Donald Trump, a former president. Trump is hoping to unseat Biden. Both have yet to be formally declared nominees by their respective parties. But the polls tell us Biden and Trump will be the probable nominees.

And then we have our guest today, Hugo McCormick, a recent entry into the presidential race as the PPP nominee. Hugo is neither a political neophyte nor a person too timid to speak his mind on what he considers important political issues. For those not familiar with PPP, it stands for Practical Party of the People.

"Mr. McCormick is a former congressman from Connecticut and until recently a syndicated columnist with *The Hartford Globe*. He has taken a leave of absence to enter the race for the White House. His views on just about everything controversial have been publicized in his editorials, speeches, and a book he recently published called, *No More Small Talk*. I've known him for years. He is a man with lots to say and a reputation for saying it. Welcome to our program, Mr. McCormick. Good to see you again."

"Thanks for having me, Alistair. As you know, I go by Hugo."

"OK, Hugo, let's get to it. I want to discuss your decision to run for the presidency. At one point we had ten to twelve candidates from the two major parties seeking to be elected. Now, unless something unexpected occurs, only Joe Biden, Donald Trump, and you are the probable nominees. Maybe Senator Manchin will run as the nominee of a party recently formed—I believe it's called No Labels Party. So why are you running for the presidency?"

"That's a fair question, Alistair. As you know, I was elected to the House in 2002 as an Independent Party candidate. I left Congress after two terms in office. I decided not to seek re-election, because as an Independent, I was ineffectual. I had the drive, ideas, and proposals, but no listeners."

"Yes, but why run for the presidency now?" said Alistair. "You had your opportunity in Washington."

"I'm getting there," said Hugo, "but just a bit slower. As you know, from a realistic point of view, we have a two-party political system. Over the past 100 years, in every presidential election either the Democrat or Republican nominee is elected president. Most Democrat and Republican registered voters typically vote the party line.

"Some such registered voters might be influenced to vote for a nominee solely by what a nominee might say on a specific matter, like abortion, gun control, immigration and the like. Typically, most voters are not aware of the views of nominees on most matters of significant importance to our country or how a nominee will address such important matters if elected.

"I blame the nominees for not discussing the critical issues the next president will need to address and for letting voters know how they will address critical issues. I blame the voters for not demanding more information from the nominees."

"What do you mean by that?" said Alistair.

Hugo paused for a moment, then said "Party nominees prefer not to have serious dialogue on matters of national and international importance. Why not? That's because views typically result in controversy—and controversy results in the possible loss of votes from citizens who might not agree with the nominee's views. Most voters don't know or seem to care how a nominee will address important national and global concerns, if elected. The result is party-line voting."

"So you think, regardless of who is chosen as the nominee by the Democratic or Republican party, it really doesn't matter to most voters because they tend to vote along party lines, rather than on what a nominee will do when elected?" asked Alistair.

"That's right," said Hugo. "In presidential elections, voters, if they are going to vote at all, tend to vote along party lines. Registered Democrats typically vote for the Democrat nominee. Registered Republicans typically vote for the Republican nominee. It's the unaffiliated or Independent Party voters who influence the outcome of elections. And if an unaffiliated voter is not happy with the choices for a president, they either won't vote … or will vote for the candidate they find least objectionable. That's the way the system works and has been working for years. It's a system which too often produces a president not worthy of the position."

"I need to press you on this, Hugo. Let's be more specific," said Alistair. "For example, let's take Healthcare. From my chair it looks like all the candidates talk about their views on Healthcare."

"True, but what's being said? Our present healthcare system is expensive, broken, and needs fixing. This is not a partisan matter. Both nominees have expressed the need to make changes to transform the way healthcare is delivered. Republicans favor a system that allows the consumer to make their own health care decisions, relying on tax credits or rebates to fund the purchase of private sector plans. Democrats favor universal Federal coverage with government-operated insurance plans competing with private plans, a system not too far removed from a nationalized healthcare system.

"Everyone agrees that healthcare needs to be addressed by the next president. But what specific changes are being proposed by the nominees? None, that I'm aware of, but I've put the details of my proposed healthcare plan on the table for all to see."

"What other things are Biden and Trump not talking about?" asked Alistair.

"Immigration! Lots of talk here, but the current administration has made a mess of our immigration policies. Simply stated, our country is being swamped by illegal immigrants entering through our southern borders. We have border patrol personnel, but little border control. Once an illegal immigrant enters our country, they're permitted to stay. We feed them, give them a place to stay, and provide healthcare to those needing medical attention. We don't know who these immigrants are, where they will go once here, or why they chose to come to the United States.

"Are we not nurturing the growth of terrorist cell groups that someday might threaten our lifestyles? Are illegal immigrants intentionally invited into our country with the expectation that someday they will support politicians seeking elective office? I hope not.

"I'm for closing our borders to all immigrants until we have in place controls to block those who are not legally permitted to be here. Restrictive controls prohibiting illegal immigrants should not be difficult to implement. In fact, we already have prohibitive controls in place. They're just not being enforced."

"Anything else?" asked Alistair.

"Crime, gangs, drugs—have any of the other nominees proposed plans addressing the rising crime rate, preventing trafficking of drugs, or arresting persons involved as part of those disorganized gangs who ruthlessly loot and damage retail stores in our towns and cities?

"Other crucial areas requiring presidential leadership are our involvement in the Middle-East conflict, the Russia-Ukraine war, our energy needs and sources, and our space program. What are the other nominees saying about these concerns? It doesn't matter which side of the political aisle a nominee sits, these concerns beg for non-partisan dialogue and action. Why aren't these matters front and center on all political agendas? Am I the only nominee who sees the importance of addressing these matters?"

"Is that all," said Alistair.

"No, that's not all. Perhaps the biggest area of concern, one rarely discussed by politicians, is the increasing disparity in incomes among the *haves* and *have-nots*. It's not necessarily the disparity in incomes that's the problem—it's the insufficient income being earned by the lower-paid workers. They need financial motivation to rise above reliance on entitlement programs. Our financial reward system is out of whack.

"Should corporate CEOs continue to reward themselves with excessive compensation packages, say annual net incomes in excess of thirty million—incomes that make a mockery out of the concept of a fair day's pay for a fair day's work? Should entertainers earn incomes of over two hundred million dollars a year? Look at the pricy contracts offered to the elite among professional athletes. Many are paid more than one hundred million a year to play a game. Just last month it was reported that Jon Rahm, a professional golfer, signed a six hundred million-dollar contract just to switch from playing golf on the PGA tour to playing golf on the LIV tour.

"I don't want to be considered a person with socialistic views, but a capitalist society such as ours won't remain much longer if we don't provide a better path for lower wage earners to share in the American Dream. I have a plan to motivate the *have-nots* to become *haves*.

"I think you get my point. These issues are important and need to be addressed by the nominees to give voters a better basis upon which to vote. I'm hoping my candidacy will encourage voters to demand that nominees speak out on these same issues."

"OK, Hugo. Let's talk about the other nominees," said Alistair. "No doubt you don't have a high opinion of them."

"I didn't say that, Alistair. In fact, I respect both for what they represent. They're educated, politically savvy, skilled public speakers, faithful to their own beliefs, and love their country. But is that enough to qualify one to be president? I don't think so. Shouldn't we know what to expect from a person who wants to lead our country for the next four years? Will the nominees make decisions that are best for our country, as opposed to the best interests of themselves, their party, or special interest groups?"

"How about age?" asked Alistair. "Biden's 81 and Trump's not far behind."

"I didn't bring tap shoes, Alistair, so I won't dance around the issue. Should age be an issue? Certainly not! Will age be an issue?

You bet—but not by me. I'm no spring chicken either. Neither are you. So age is a factor I'll leave for others to assess. I've read reports that Biden has experienced episodes of mild senility and that four more years might be a difficult stretch for him. And I've read reports that Trump's personality has changed in the past few years so that his age might be the cause of him becoming too self-centered, impulsive, and paranoid—characteristics often associated with people his age. I'll go no further on this issue."

"We have only a few moments left, Hugo. Could you sum up why you are more qualified to be president of the United States than either Biden or Trump?" queried Alistair.

"I'm not saying I would be a better president than any of my opponents. I am saying that there are more important issues to consider when electing a president than age, party affiliation, promises, or a nominee's position on an isolated issue, such as abortion, gun control, or immigration.

"The right to vote is important, but more important is that the vote be based on a reasonable evaluation of the character, qualifications, beliefs, and capabilities of the presidential nominees. My beliefs and positions on important concerns are well documented. I challenge my opponents to let the voters know who they really are, why they are qualified to lead and manage our country, and what they will do if elected. The voters should demand no less from all the nominees."

Alistair acknowledged the signal that it was almost twelve. "Hugo, thanks for being my guest on *Face the Press*. Your thoughts are provoking, and I wouldn't have expected less. That's all for today. We'll be back next Sunday. I'm Alistair MacDougal and this is *Face the Press*."

⟳★⟲

CHAPTER 35

Campaigning Out West
2/2/2024—2/16/2024

★ ★ ★

Hugo's wife and two daughters, Kim and Kris, accompanied Hugo as they boarded a chartered flight from Bradley International Airport to Denver, Colorado.

Louise anticipated hitting the campaign trail as she was aware that presidential candidates' spouses could substantially affect the outcome of an election. Public appearances were easy for Louise. As a former high school principal, she was not uncomfortable speaking in public, and could be counted on to say the right things.

Kim and Kris on the other hand initially didn't like the publicity and fanfare they were receiving as daughters of a possible president. However, whatever shyness they initially possessed soon dissipated after public appearances by them became routine. In fact, it didn't take long before both looked forward to more of the attention they were receiving.

Koko Shaw, their father's new campaign manager, asked that Kim and Kris become more involved in their father's campaign to recruit volunteers, but cautioned them about trying to interpret what their father was saying. Koko and Macey flew to Denver earlier in the week to meet with local staffers to coordinate events for Hugo during his visit.

This was a big trip for Hugo—an important trip, because Hugo had not made any prior campaign visits to West Coast states, and he feared his lack of presence might send the wrong message.

His schedule had him in Denver for a day and a half, then to Santa Fe, New Mexico for a day, two days in Phoenix, two days in L.A, a day in Sacramento, a day in Salem, Oregon, a night in Boise, Idaho, two days in Salt Lake City, a luncheon in Cheyenne, and then back to Denver for a day before returning to Connecticut. His wife and daughters planned to sightsee in areas where Hugo would be campaigning.

On February 16th the chartered flight began the return trip to Hartford. Koko and Macey joined Hugo and his family for the return trip, giving Hugo an opportunity to assess the value of the trip. Macey couldn't wait to express his feelings about the trip. After taking a seat next to Koko and across from Hugo, he began the conversation by saying; "I've never seen so many enthusiastic crowds. They like you, Hugo. They like your candid, no-nonsense approach to communicating your views."

"It's not me, Macey. It's the message," said Hugo. "You and your staffers deserve the applause. Great job on the scheduling. You put together a rock-solid organization. But that's what you said you'd do."

"The credit really should go to Liz and Crystal. And it wouldn't hurt if you told them so," said Macey.

"I will, Mace." After what seemed like a minute of silence, Hugo then said "How about you, Koko? Do you think I have a chance?"

"I couldn't be more pleased. I like your chances. The press could have been kinder. But so what! The media has favorites and will taint reporting facts accordingly. Forget them. The people vote, and the people are sending a loud and clear message. They don't want Biden or Trump. They like you. And they should. You're giving them a real solid alternative to *politics as usual.* You didn't mince words. Increased disposal income for hard-working families, sensible immigration controls, peace in the Mideast and in the world, solutions to gangs and crime in our streets—all concerns that relate to persons of all ages, races and genders. Don't get too overconfident—there's a long way to go, but support for your values and goals are mushrooming."

Hugo felt good. So did Macey. Things were going better than expected. In fact, too good. But Koko was aware of a little problem.

Halfway through the flight, when Koko and Hugo were alone in the back of the plane, Koko said, "Hugo, take a peek at what one of the Denver staffers handed me as I was getting on the plane. There's an article about you in *National Rumors*—and you're on the cover."

"What the hell is National Rumors?" said Hugo.

"One of those gossip magazines that sensationalize anything to attract readers. You're a public figure," said Koko. "You're news. Rumors sell publications. And rumors can be an effective tool to tarnish a person's image. We can't ignore what was written. It could have a ripple effect unless we snip it right away. Is there any truth to these accusations?"

CHAPTER 36

Smear Tactics,
A First for Hugo
2/16/2024

★ ★ ★

The plane was 45 minutes from Bradley International Airport. Hugo angrily grabbed the magazine from Koko's hand and shook his head in disbelief. He again looked at the picture and caption on the front page, and then turned to page 17 to read the article. He couldn't believe what he was reading. He had just been set up by professional mudslingers.

"Son of a bitch," said Hugo. "Looks like I finally made the big leagues."

Hugo decided it best to explain the article to his family in the privacy of the plane. He called his wife and daughters over to the table, and spread the cover of the magazine in front of them. "Looks like you should be aware of something. That's my picture on the front page. Must have been taken back in 2005 or 2006."

The picture suggested Hugo to be a man he truly wasn't. The caption intimated Hugo did things while in Congress other than tend to business. Underneath the picture of Hugo and his attractive, well-endowed red head companion, in bold yellow and red glossy print, was the caption: "Is Hugo suffering from Bill Clinton's disease?"

Kim and Kris were visibly upset. So was Louise—not because of the article, but because she knew someone was toying with Hugo's head and reputation. "What are they saying about you, Dad?" said Kris. "Who's the girl?"

The article was less provocative than the photo caption. "Someone took a picture of me years ago at a cocktail party in Washington. That's me having a drink with a friend who accompanied me to the party. Name's Aleysha. She's not a call girl."

Looking at Kim and Kris, Hugo said, "Your mom and I were in the process of getting a divorce at the time. We had been living separate lives for a few years. I dated a few times in Washington, and this was one of those times. No big deal."

"Then why is someone bringing this up now," said Kim.

"Well, the divorce was not final—so now someone wants to label me as an unfaithful who can't be trusted."

"Dad, is she the reason why you and mom got divorced?" said Kim.

"No, No," said Hugo. "Your mom and I hadn't been getting along for years. Probably my fault because I left her alone for long periods. She didn't like the idea that I left my law practice for a job in Congress. She never wanted me to be a politician. After I got elected, she vowed never to join me in Washington. And she never did. I spent as much time as I could at home, but apparently not enough. I flew home one day to surprise her on her birthday. She was surprised all right. So was I. She wasn't as lonely as I had thought. She had been enjoying cocktails with a friend, Lou Vitto, my law partner. I'll spare the details, but it was apparent they were more than just friends."

"Why didn't you tell us," said Kris.

"I would if I had to," said Hugo. "But I didn't have to. You both were young, so your mother and I decided to make it appear we were divorced for reasons of incompatibility. In a way, that was the reason. But now you know there was more to it. I could have caused a stink and embarrassed a few people, including myself, but we decided it would be in everyone's best interest to have a quick and quiet divorce. I let your mom keep the house and I gave her a few bucks. I moved out just after the divorce and moved to Madison. That's where I met Louise."

"So, what's the big deal then?" said Kris. "You and mom no longer were a couple."

"Shouldn't be a big deal, Kris," said Koko. "But the press will make it an issue unless your father sets the record straight. It needs to be explained."

CHAPTER 37

Trip Downtown
3/15/2024

★ ★ ★

March 15th is Spring Break at Duke, which was very easy to tell. The parking lot was empty, except for Justin's car and a few bikes. Many students returned home to see their parents and friends. Others left for Myrtle Beach, Hilton Head, or to beach towns in Florida or the Bahamas. A few students remained on campus. Tikes Diner in Durham experienced a substantial drop in business during spring breaks, so Justin was planning on closing the diner early.

Shortly after six, while he was cleaning up inside, four black Ford Expeditions with flashing blue lights pulled up outside Tike's front door. Eight people exited the vehicles. Six took positions outside the diner, blocking the entrance, while another two entered the diner and approached Justin.

"Are you Justin Alabi?" demanded Captain Brittany, who was in charge. He flashed a bronze-plated badge that stated, "Captain Brittany, FBI."

Justin stared at the two men, hoping what he had feared for a long time was not actually happening. "Yes, sir, I'm Justin. What can I do for you?"

"We want to ask you a few questions, Justin. You'll have to come with us."

"Wait a minute," bellowed Justin. "What for? What did I do?"

"Just come with us. We have a few questions to ask."

"What if I don't want to go?" challenged Justin.

"We need you to come with us, Justin. We prefer not to make a scene."

"I'm the only one here," said Justin. "At least let me close the diner."

Justin left the counter a mess, turned off the lights, and locked the door. He was placed in the back seat of Captain Brittany's vehicle. Then the four vehicles proceeded to the downtown office of the FBI.

The trip only took five minutes, which was just enough time for Justin's mind to race through tons of unpleasant thoughts. He wondered whether his name came up in any terrorist plots. Or maybe he would be questioned about his meeting with Professor Ibala. He contemplated nothing but the worst results from this trip downtown.

CHAPTER 38

Campaign Assessment
4/5/2024

★ ★ ★

Koko Shaw had worked on both Republican and Democrat congressional campaigns for over 25 years. He took a breather from the Biden—Trump 2020 presidential campaigns, and though requested, turned down positions with both parties. But when asked if he would engineer Hugo's efforts to be elected, Koko couldn't resist accepting the position of campaign manager—a position which Macey was glad to be relieved.

Macey was successful in getting Hugo to run, but realized it was only a matter of time before the campaign had to hire a few heavy hitters. Joe Buck, who signed on a few months ago, had his hands full scheduling luncheons, dinners, and other appearances for Hugo. Koko and Joe had worked together on several prior occasions with no power struggles. They got along well. With Koko as the new campaign manager, Macey, Blair, Liz, and Crystal could spend more time on promoting Hugo, his platform, and his campaign messages to potential voters.

Koko didn't need a fancy office. He set up his operations on a desk in the center of several other desks in the open area on the first floor. He came on board with hands-on experience, and the necessary skills to lead a staff of 52 people, mostly younger generation college students, with no political experience. He was relying on Liz and Crystal to continue coordinating the work of the state organizations and their respective network of volunteers. Macey had told everyone connected with the campaign that Koko now would be calling all the shots—except Hugo had veto authority.

Koko scheduled a progress meeting of the campaign leaders at ten in the morning on Friday, April 5th. Joe Buck was there. So were Macey, Blair, Liz and Crystal. Justin wasn't there nor expected. Five other campaign leaders were invited, but only three could attend. Two were in Connecticut visiting Hugo to coordinate a response to the National Rumor's article, and to discuss the impact of the recent arrest of Justin Alabi. C. B. McGranahan was at the meeting representing PPP's newly appointed CPA firm, McGranahan and Levine.

Koko started the meeting by complimenting the Group of Five for putting Hugo's campaign in a high gear mode immediately after Hugo made the decision to run. He then proceeded to review the legal status of PPP, the need to formalize its objectives, the naming of a more permanent slate of officers and directors, and his expectations of the staff for the months ahead. "Times sure have changed," said Koko. "Twenty years ago, we had to pound the pavements to solicit support. Dinners and fundraisers were an everyday necessity. Door to door contact by volunteers distributing fliers destined for trash cans were part of the program, and now a thing of the past. Now we can virtually orchestrate the entire campaign from our offices here in Durham. Well done!"

Koko then commented on the status of the campaign. "What more can I say? The campaign is going great! We're getting support and positive feedback from a broad based, cross-section of previously unhappy voters. If the election were held today, I think we'd have a fair shot at winning. One national poll has Hugo trailing Biden by two percentage points and in a dead heat with Donald Trump. The latest

AOL poll shows Hugo leading both Biden and Trump by at least three percentage points. I like the AOL poll!

"Let's go around the table," said Koko. "Joe, why don't you start. What's Hugo's schedule for next month?"

Joe leaned forward in his chair with arms on the table, right arm on top of his left. He looked around the table to assess the interest of those who were present, then proceeded to say what he had to say. "As you all know, Hugo has been kept quite busy the past two months with visits to about 15 states, luncheon speeches in Hilton Head and Atlanta, fundraising dinners in New York, Philadelphia and Washington, and several breakfast sessions with staff along the way. He just returned from a 15-day trip out West. As Koko has said, we are experiencing nothing but favorable feedback, both from voters and the polls. There've been a few glitches, but nothing that should impede the chances of Hugo being elected."

"What kind of glitches?" said Blair.

"Nothing we can't handle," said Joe. "National Rumors, a junk magazine, had a picture of Hugo on the front page with a caption suggesting he had been unfaithful to his prior wife while a member of Congress. Hugo's says the insinuation is absurd. He is preparing a response which should put an end to voter concerns. And you all know that Justin was picked up by the FBI recently. We don't know exactly what for, but we can handle whatever might develop. In the meantime, I suggest we distance ourselves from Justin until we know why he was arrested.

"We have a few things planned for Hugo in the coming weeks. I've been having discussions with our Massachusetts supporters and a luncheon engagement is scheduled next Wednesday at Quincy Market's Nathanial Hall in Boston. Quincy Market typically is crowded during lunch time. So, we plan to have microphones which will broadcast his speech from inside Nathanial Hall to an outdoor crowd in the immediate area. Hugo's looking forward to this event as he realizes he has spent little time campaigning in the Northeast and has some catching up to do. He plans to talk about the problems in the Mideast and immigration, two issues which people in the area seem concerned."

"How about Connecticut?" said Koko. "That's his home state."

"Agree," said Joe. "Hugo knows the political personalities in Connecticut on a first name basis. Most of the politicians already are committed to either Biden or Trump, so we are avoiding contact with them. We've already make stops last December in several Connecticut cities, but are planning to make appearances in Hartford, New Haven, and Stamford within the next two weeks. Our Connecticut staffers are working on details as we speak. Connecticut will not be overlooked."

"Anything we can do to help?" said Macey.

"Just keep our volunteers and supporters informed and motivated," said Joe. "And we can always use more money, particularly as we get closer to next November."

Macey, Liz and Crystal followed with comments on operational aspects of the campaign. Crystal said they were experiencing a problem which really isn't a problem—too many volunteers. "We don't blow them off," said Crystal. "We put many on hold, telling them they will be contacted if a need arises, but encouraging them to establish their own online events to further support the campaign. It's surprising how many volunteers and donors from across the country have responded by just a few clicks of a mouse. If I had to guess, I'd say we have over three hundred thousand volunteers from Internet solicitations."

Campaign funding was the next issue to be discussed. Blair continued in charge of donors and campaign funding—with the financial assistance from C. B. McGranahan and his CPA firm. "We have been actively soliciting donor funds for approximately five months," said Blair. "Our elaborate state networks have implemented online funding vehicles which have produced over 140 million dollars from contributions of 500 dollars or less. Each donor is being asked to further support Hugo by requesting others to donate. At this rate we will be overfunded—not a bad situation. C.B. has assured me our financial records are intact."

"They are," said C.B. "Blair and his staff have done an excellent job. We have an airtight compliance system with which no regulatory authorities should find fault."

CHAPTER 39

Zack's Limo Services

★ ★ ★

Zackary and Bub Hyde, brothers who lived in Connecticut, owned Zack's Limo Service LLC. Zack lived on State Street in Guilford and Bub lived in West Haven. The business was located in Westwood's Plaza, a small shopping center on Route 1 in Guilford, Connecticut—South of Bishop's Farm. The business operated out of a small two-room office with enough parking in the rear for three black, stretch limousines.

Zack's furnished transportation services throughout Connecticut and bordering states. Three part-time employees of Zack's worked alternating days between the hours of nine to five, seven days a week. Their primary responsibilities were to answer phones, book services, and do the bookkeeping. Zack and Bub did most of the driving, but had arrangements with three retired policemen to drive on an "on call" basis.

Zack made sure all the people who worked for him gave approval to have background checks which included driving experience, criminal records, credit history and drug use. FBI reports were obtained on all employees. Zack wanted his customers to be comfortable with the drivers who escort them.

The three limousines were less than three years old. The company's policy was to trade in a vehicle whenever the vehicle had been in use for three years. Each limousine was top of the line and came equipped with all the amenities typically found in luxury limos, including a luxury bar with snacks.

Zack's Limo Services weren't cheap, but they were efficient and reliable. The company enjoyed a reputation among its competitors and the public for being professional and courteous.

Hugo used Zack's Limo Services when traveling to speaking events in the tristate area. He had used Zack's when he gave a luncheon speech in Nathanial Hall. He used Zack's the following week when he attended functions in Hartford, New Haven, and Stamford. Zack told Hugo he and Bub would personally accompany Hugo, Louise and three members of his campaign staff to a speech Hugo would be making in Madison Square Garden on June 30th. Hugo had hired two limos from Zack's for the occasion.

CHAPTER 40

Madison Square Garden
6/30/2024

★ ★ ★

Madison Square Garden was packed with supporters, donors, members of the Press, and others who wanted to assess first-hand what Hugo was all about. The event featured several local politicians, but the main speaker was Hugo. The event was planned by Joe Buck, several PPP staffers, and others who represented candidates seeking the position of mayor of the City of New York.

Hugo viewed the event as an opportunity for him to express his thoughts on matters he considered of interest to New Yorkers. Koko and Joe Buck were among those present. Hugo gave Koko and Joe an outline of what he would be talking about, not requesting nor expecting their blessing. Preparations for the event began early February as Madison Square Garden is a difficult venue to book.

After two candidates for the mayor's position spoke to the audience, the chairman of the event signaled to Joe Buck that it was time for Hugo to speak. So, Joe proceeded to the podium to introduce Hugo.

"Greetings and thanks for showing up tonight. As you are aware, the guest speaker tonight is Hugo McCormick, a name which by now should be familiar to you. Nevertheless, I'll say a few words about him you might not know.

"Hugo is a man who was asked to step up to the plate to serve his country. For many reasons he didn't want to run for the presidency. He was happy doing what he did best, that is critiquing politicians and prodding them to get involved in problems politicians were ignoring.

"He had been hoping voters would elect a president in 2024 who would be admired and respected here in our country and abroad. He was hoping the next president had the qualifications and desire to address important matters in a non-partisan way. He was hoping the next president could work with members of Congress to eradicate the creeping culture of partisan voting on important matters that required legislative action.

"Though he didn't want to run for the presidency, in his view, the applicants for the job, Joe Biden and Donald Trump, did not measure up to the qualifications the position of president requires. We need a leader—not a talker. We need a person with no political ax to grind. We need a person who won't blink when confronted with difficult issues requiring presidential action. We need a person who will administer and manage in a non-partisan manner so that government action on matters requiring legislative approval will not become stymied by partisan gerrymandering. We need a person capable of working with leaders from other countries to find solutions to global threats to mankind. Well, here he is—a person who I think you will agree is the one best qualified for the job of president of the United States, Hugo."

The crowd gave Hugo a warm reception. Applause was accompanied by scattered chants of *No More Small Talk – No More Small Talk*. After the crowd settled, Hugo began speaking. "Thank you for being here tonight. Believe me, I'm humbled by the turnout." Hugo continued by personally thanking those responsible for coordinating the event and the many volunteers involved in making the event happen. He told the audience he would limit his remarks to topics he thought all nominees for the presidency should address.

Hugo understood speaking in Madison Square Garden on the topic of the Israeli—Palestinian conflict in the Mideast to an audience with many Jews and Palestinians might prove to be a bit testy. And if he were to express his view on the need for a two-state solution to the territorial dispute, he might provoke uncontrolled yelling and screaming among those with differing views.

But Hugo thought a permanent solution was needed between the two if a path to global peace was possible, and that the president of the United States should be an important player in the process. So, Hugo, exercising caution, began the formal part of his speech by saying, "We must find a permanent and peaceful solution to the long-standing differences between the Israelis and the Palestinians over territorial rights. Our world will never see global peace until both agree on a two-state solution whereby both countries live in harmony in separate but contiguous homelands." Hugo went on to say he thought most Jews and Palestinians had similar cultural beliefs and lifestyles, had been living and working together in the region for years, and that it shouldn't be a giant leap to agree on definitive territorial boundaries. He did point out that he was aware there were Arab groups with radical Islamic beliefs that called for the extinction of Israelis from the former Palestine territories and worldwide, and that such radical beliefs had to be modified if peace in the area and on our planet ever was to be achieved.

Hugo was not naïve. He wisely decided not to express his thoughts concerning who he thought owned what and where in the region. Rather, his message to the audience was pure and simple—"A permanent peace between the Israelis and Palestinians is achievable but will never be accomplished without a compromise by both parties to the control of the territories in dispute. Hugo proceeded to say what he would do toward consummating a compromise if he were elected president.

Hugo, not wanting to incite certain elements within the attending crowd, cautiously changed the subject to the rise in crimes and gangs in our cities, the need to find out the reasons why, and then deal with the reasons. "We can't accept living in a society where it's unsafe to take a walk in the park or shop in stores." Hugo said he didn't have all the answers, but did recognize the existing chaos in the cities. He promised to do something about it if elected.

Hugo then talked about Income Disparity and the legislation he would recommend to increase the purchasing power of low-income persons so that they could live a life without relying on government entitlements. He pointed out that he expressed his thoughts on income disparity in detail in his book, *No More Small Talk*, and that the contents of the book could be downloaded free from his website NMST2023@aol.com.

Hugo commented on a few other concerns he thought were of interest to New Yorkers—then ended his speech at 9:20 with a standing ovation from the crowd. There were a few scattered chants from patriotic Jews and Palestinians, but overall Koko and Joe were pleased with the way Hugo handled some real tough issues.

Hugo had wanted to remain and mingle among the crowd, but Joe and his campaign assistants thought otherwise and hustled Hugo and Louise through a side door exit of the Garden and into the rear of the second of two black stretch limousines awaiting the departure of Hugo, Louise, and his campaign staff. The limo drivers had instructions to drive Hugo and his wife back to Essex, Connecticut, and to drive the campaign staff to Stamford, Connecticut where they would spend the night.

CHAPTER 41

Memorial Service,
Madison Congregational Church
7/10/2024

★ ★ ★

Kim   ***Kris***

The setting was magnificent. The mood was somber. The church was overflowing.

Madison Congregational Church is located just to the rear of the Madison Green on the Boston Post Road, in Madison, Connecticut. Hugo and Louise were married at this church almost 15 years ago on July 4th, 2009. Louise wanted the memorial service to be held at the church at which they were married. Kim and Kris agreed.

Louise wanted a traditional coffin burial, which would allow putting into the coffin pictures of Kim and Kris with their father and a few of their father's cherished possessions, including his Connecticut License Plate, NMST. The gold wedding band that said Louise and

Hugo, 7/4/2009 would remain on Hugo's left hand. The casket, pictures, and personal items all were to be buried with Hugo in a plot at the Riverside Cemetery in Essex, Connecticut. Neither Hugo nor Louise expressed in their wills a desire to be cremated.

It was ten in the morning. The parking area was jammed. The persons who wanted to pay tribute to Hugo came from all walks of life and from many miles away. Kim planned to speak on behalf of the remaining family. Koko Shaw, campaign manager and friend of Hugo's for over twenty years, responded favorably to the family's request that he deliver the eulogy honoring Hugo. The service was planned to last about an hour.

President Biden and ex-president Donald Trump didn't attend, but sent flowers and personal messages to Louise, Kim, and Kris. Jack Lambert and his wife were there. So was Joe Buck and the members of the Group of Five, including Justin. Professor Crum attended and wanted to make a few comments, but time constraints limited his role to being a spectator. Louise's mother was there in a wheelchair. Maureen McCormick Vitti attended the service with her second husband and Hugo's ex-law partner, Lou Vitti. Kim's husband, Mike, was seated alongside Kim, Louise, Kris and her husband, Scott, in the front row.

Bishop Lawson, a high school friend of Hugo's, began the service by thanking all those who attended. He commented generally on how much Hugo had meant to him and his family. Bishop Lawson had been asked by Louise to read a passage from the Bible which had great significance to Hugo. After reading the passage, the bishop introduced Kim, who wanted to say a few words to her father.

Kim at one time never would have stood up in front of so many people to speak. But the election experience had given her sufficient courage to say a few words while her father was still in the room. Somewhat out of character for Kim, the passage of almost ten days since the death of her father justified Kim wearing a black business suit and a yellow rose firmly attached to her light bronze frizzled hair. Her dress suggested she had accepted the death of her father. Now she had to get on with her life. Her demeanor suggested his life would not be easy to forget.

"Kris and I are here only because we must be, and not because this is the way we wanted to share our last words with our father. We know him as Pop. You know him as Hugo. So, I will say a few last words to Pop, hoping he is still among us and listening to what I have to say.

"Pop, while you were alive, I never told you how much I appreciated all the things you did for me throughout my life. As I look back, all the sacrifices you made for me while growing up, I took for granted. All the times you sat down with me and listened to my thoughts, concerns, and problems, and then helped me figure things out, I took for granted. All the school plays, soccer games, tennis matches, parties, and graduations you attended or found time to take me to, I took for granted. All the family vacations and holidays which you went out of your way to make sure I had fond memories, I took for granted. The many times you allowed me to make my own decisions even though you had to bite your tongue at times, I took for granted. All the times I needed help, and you offered help without asking questions, I took for granted. And the times you let me drive the family car, make my own choice about attending college, and allowed me to think I was choosing my own friends and my own way of life, I took for granted. Only now after you're gone have I been able to appreciate the things you've done—not once asking for a thanks in return. I hope it's not too late for you to hear me now say, thanks, Pop! I won't forget you."

Kim stood behind the podium for what seemed to be a long moment of silence—tears were freely flowing down her cheeks. The audience remained silent as she slowly walked from the podium and sat down next to her husband. Louise and Kris struggled to hold back tears. Many in the audience couldn't.

After a brief pause, Koko approached the podium. Koko was no stranger to speaking in public, but he wasn't accustomed to giving eulogies for close friends. His eyes became humid while Kim was speaking. But he restrained his emotions so that only he knew the extent to which he had been emotionally impacted.

"Kim, those were moving thoughts about your Pop. I'm sure he heard them—and if you close your eyes and listen carefully, I think you'll hear a voice whispering from above, 'Thanks.' "

Koko paused for ten seconds to allow the mood to change gear. Then he continued. "I want to say a few words about the Hugo I know. I have known him for over 20 years, as a lawyer, a congressman, a journalist, a presidential contender—but more importantly as a person with whom I was able to share personal thoughts. He was a person with compassion, a person who always found time for friends, a person who you could count on if you needed help. Indeed, he was my friend.

"Prior to October last year, Hugo had no thoughts of becoming a presidential candidate. He had his taste of politics when he was elected to Congress years ago. I was his campaign manager back then. He left Congress after four years in office, disappointed in his inability to accomplish anything meaningful. Once out of office, he found his niche as a political journalist working for The Hartford Globe. His editorials became syndicated to the major newspapers. As most of you know, he attained a high level of popularity as a journalist, speaker, and author of a new book. He would speak out on political issues and solutions too often ignored by politicians. He was a voice for the many people who felt disenfranchised by the politicians for whom they voted.

"Hugo was not a boisterous person. He didn't have to scream or shout to be heard. He wasn't audacious or rude. Rather, he was a reticent person who liked to see things done right. He was not a man who would hide in the crowd. He was passionate in his beliefs. When he had something to say, he'd say it without mincing words. People close to him knew he wore no labels on his character or beliefs. If he had a fault, it was that he had no patience for political pandering. He respected politicians for what the system made them, but felt that those seeking political office too often neglect the concerns of their constituents.

"Hugo had the vision to identify the many social and economic issues of our times. He wanted political candidates to address issues that were meaningful to our country, so that voters when entering the ballot box would know something about the persons on the presidential ballot. It upset him to see that year after year voters would cast votes knowing little about the person they're voting for. This year was no different. He didn't like the fact that the 2024 presidential election was shaping up to be between two veteran politicians who preferred to run campaigns based on personalities, age, empty promises, and negative campaigning.

"Often Hugo angered people. Sometimes his proposals were not popular. But when Hugo was convinced something needed fixing, he thought people should know what was wrong, why, and how it could be fixed. He didn't avoid talking about issues most politicians dared not consider. In this regard, Hugo was not afraid to talk freely about the Israel and Palestinian religious and territorial differences, or Russia's invasion into Ukraine's territory, or the income insufficiency of those striving to rise above the near poverty level to share in the American dream. He was not afraid to talk about religion and how certain religious fanatics might affect world peace by refusing to accept the concept of religious diversity. He was not afraid to talk about legalizing drugs if the legalization of drugs was the best approach to combat drug related crimes and gangs. He was not afraid to talk about the need for tax relief for lower income persons if tax relief would motivate those lower income persons to cease relying on government hand out programs. And he was not afraid to talk about the importance of our space program and the need for all countries to recognize that no one country should be able to exclusively control the space above our Earth.

"We don't know why Hugo died so suddenly. We can speculate, but we may never know. We do know that his demanding schedule might have had a straining impact on his physical condition. We also know there were voices here and abroad who sharply differed with his approach to handling several controversial matters, such as how he planned to eliminate the territorial differences between the Palestinians and the Israelis, or what he would do as president to prevent foreigners from entering our country as illegal immigrants, particularly those entering our country through our southern borders, or what steps he would advocate to eliminate the crippling effects of drugs and gang related activities in our towns and cities. Voices with opposing views would prefer that he clam up.

"We do know that the cause of his death needs investigation. We do know that during the past two months, he and his family had received threats from unknown sources threatening harm to him and his family if he didn't find a way to withdraw from his presidential run. Hugo knew there would be times when he couldn't avoid brushing up against the threshold of foul play. But he had a mission—and that was to be honest to his convictions and do what he thought was right for the country.

"We lost a good man in Hugo. He never wanted to run for the presidency. But he did feel he was anointed by someone higher up to send a message to both voters and those seeking to become our next president. I think he delivered his message.

"What would he say to us today if he could write a few parting words? I think he would write that he hoped his candidacy delivered a message to voters that the position of president of the United States requires a person with exceptional skills and talents. I think he would say that voters have an important role to play in the selection of a president, and that they should not cast a vote for a person they know little about. I think he would say that candidates for the presidency should stop bickering, bashing, and bantering, and tell voters how they will handle the important national and global issues requiring presidential leadership. Lastly, I think Hugo would say that our existing two-party political structure is not working as too often the structure produces a president through party-line voting—and election by party-line voting typically does not produce the best qualified person for the job.

"That's what I think he would write. Would he be expecting too much from voters and future presidential candidates? Maybe. But maybe not."

The coffin was carried out of the church by the pallbearers. Louise, Kim, and Kris followed behind the coffin. Then those who attended the service filed out slowly and silently as the organ quietly played a song specially written for Hugo by an admirer who preferred to remain unidentified. The song was appropriately titled: *No More Small Talk*.

About the Author

The author's birth name is Bob Fraser. He chose the name Scottie Fraser as his pen name and author of his books. Why? So that anyone who disagreed with anything said in any of his five books could do battle with Scottie – and not Bob.

So, Scottie was born and raised in the town, now city, of West Haven, Connecticut. He has fond memories of old friends and memorable times while growing up in West Haven.

Now a super-senior, Scottie and his wife, Barbara, raised four children in the town of Guilford, Connecticut. The children now are off on their own, all with families that have made Scottie and his wife grandparents to nine grandchildren.

Scottie graduated from West Haven High School, Duke University, and University of Connecticut School of Law—spending a couple of years in the military before attending law school. He was involved during his working career as a lawyer, banker, investor, developer, and in a few other areas he now can't remember—but never as a writer or author. Now retired, he represents to others that he is an author. Many of his close acquaintances might dispute this characterization.

Scottie also penned books on politics, golf, seafood, and humor. His books are listed on Amazon.com/scottiefraser. His email address is erfraser@aol.com.